A Eucharist Sourcebook

The Sourcebook Series:

A Eucharist Sourcebook

compiled by
J. Robert Baker
Barbara Budde

LITURGY
TRAINING
PUBLICATIONS

Acknowledgments

We are grateful to the many authors and publishers who have given permission to include their work. Every effort has been made to determine the ownership of all texts and to make proper arrangements for their use. Any oversight that may have occurred, if brought to our attention, will gladly be corrected in future editions.

Acknowledgments will be found in the endnotes. Permission to reprint any texts in this book must be obtained from the copyright owners.

Acquisitions editor: Victoria M. Tufano
Production/Permissions editor: Theresa Houston
Editorial assitance: Lorraine Schmidt
Production Artist: James Mellody-Pizzato
Series design format: Michael Tapia
Photos on pages i, 1, 4, 7, 13, 21, 26, 29, 31, 35, 47, 50, 59, 62, 73, 77, 82, 86, 88, 94, 97, 101, 106, 109, 112, 115, 119 and 122 by Antonio Pérez.
Photos on pages 40, 65 and 103 © Eileen Crowley-Horak.
Photos on pages 10, 23, 55 and 91 © Bill Wittman.
Photos on pages iii, 16, 70 and 125 from Artstock.
All photos electronically manipulated by M. Urgo.

A EUCHARIST SOURCEBOOK © 1999, Archdiocese of Chicago: Liturgy Training Publications, 1800 North Hermitage Avenue, Chicago IL 60622-1101; 1-800-933-1800; orders@ltp.org; fax 1-800-933-7094. All rights reserved.

Printed in the United States of America

06 05 04 03 02 01 00 99   5 4 3 2 1

Library of Congress Cataloging-in-Publications Data
A Eucharist sourcebook / compiled by J. Robert Baker, Barbara Budde.
      p.   cm. — (The Sourcebook series)
    1. Lord's Supper — Quotations, maxims, etc. I. Baker, J. Robert, 1954– . II. Budde, Barbara. III. Series: Sourcebook series (Liturgy Training Publications)
    PN6084.L565E93   1999
234'.163 — dc21   98-49838
                                                      CIP

ISBN 1-56854-182-1
EUCHSB

Contents

Introduction

It is difficult to speak adequately of the eucharist, because seeming opposites intersect in this great sacrament of the table. It is both thing and action, person and event, meal and sacrifice, gathering and dismissal. In it, the individual and the community find healing grace and the insistent demand that they in turn offer the same to others in their everyday lives. The eucharist holds the presence of God and the mystery of life, death, and resurrection. Even though at different times Christians have stressed one aspect of the sacrament over another, it is the places where these aspects intersect that we have attempted to highlight here. Our emphasis has been on the action of the eucharist as a congregation consecrates the sacrament and as the sacrament sanctifies the congregation, both at liturgy and in the world.

We partake in the eucharist because we are hungry. Ours is an elemental hungering. We want sustenance. We crave nourishment beyond the food and drink that sustain our physical lives. We hunger for life to be spiritually meaningful and for it to be redeemed from the evil and viciousness that all too often mar it. Our hunger is the human appetite to be in communion with one another. Like the thirst of which the psalmist spoke so long ago, it is also our inescapable longing for God.

In our hunger, we gather to celebrate the eucharist. We arrive one person at a time, but we gather together in the ritual. We reflect the banquet feasts of the gospel, where the greatest and the least are welcome. Like wheat kneaded into a loaf and grapes crushed into wine, we mix into a single fellowship. In fact, as much as wheat and grape, we are the harvest out of which the eucharist is made.

Our gathering is marked by prayers of praise, thanksgiving and intercession. We praise and thank God for all the gifts that God has poured out on us and continues to give us. We offer petitions for ourselves, our families, our communities and our world.

In our prayer, we remember deeply the mystery of our paschal faith and its pledge of eternal glory. As we remember, we enter the saving action of God, which holds together past, present and future in the eternal now of God's grace. In remembering, we embrace the cross, empty tomb and final resurrection, and are shaped into Christ.

So, we offer up the gifts that we have — of bread and wine and ourselves. We offer ourselves with Christ who gave himself that all in the world might experience the fullness of life. Our oblation is a sacrifice that requires our exertion, discipline, and attention. To offer and become the wheat of the elect, we must struggle against our inclination toward divisiveness. To take up the chalice of benediction, we must discipline ourselves to love. We must be unequivocally attentive to the offering we make and to the offering that is made of us.

Because the eucharist is also eating and drinking, we celebrate as much as we sacrifice. We take comfort and pleasure in the conviviality of this sacrament. God, who has mothered us in baptism, continues to feed and nourish us with life and love in this sacred meal. Each of us comes to feast on food that has no equal. We taste the bread from heaven, the bread of angels, the bread of life. We drink the wine of nourishment from the cup of salvation. Though each of us comes to the eucharistic table and eats from it as an individual, we come forward in a procession of our fellows, here and now, past and present. We eat from a common plate and drink from a common cup. In doing so, we find ourselves deeply intimate and connected with the God who feeds us and with all those who have come forward in this and every eucharist. In this eating and drinking, we are made one with God, and we become what we eat — the Body of Christ.

As the sacrament folds us more deeply into the reality of ourselves as members of the Body of Christ, we begin to feel its curative effect. When the Maronite litany describes the sacrament as the medicine of immortality, it savors the healing that the sacrament effects. The sacrament is a cordial, strengthening the bond of charity. It is both remedy and preventive for sin. It is the curative that transforms our lives and our very selves. The gift of bread and wine transformed into the body and blood of Christ transforms us, healing sin, division and hatred.

Eucharist is certainly about how the Holy Spirit transforms mere bread and wine into the very presence of Christ, but it is also how the Holy Spirit overflows these gifts, transforming us into the life-giving sacrament for the world. In this great prayer, we who receive God's life-giving gift are converted into God's gift to the world. We who receive the eucharist are changed ourselves into the sign of God's life and love to the world. The healing grace of the eucharist demands that we feed the world. Our reception of the sacrament commits us to be bread broken and wine poured out for the world.

Many people have given us generous help in the preparation of this book. We are thankful to Martin L. Bond, John G. Budde, David M. Hammond, Gabe Huck, John P. Hussey, Anne B. Parks, Gail Ramshaw, Virginia Sloyan, Richard Sonnenshein, Jack C. Wills, and others who generously suggested materials for this book. We are appreciative of the access that Donald Sawyer, the Eucharistic Missionaries of St. Dominic, and the Paulist community of Austin, Texas, gave us to their libraries. We are also grateful for the unfailing help that John Burke, Bart Hollingsworth, and Janet Salvati provided with obtaining materials through interlibrary loan.

To borrow Flannery O'Connor's words, we offer this book as a very minor hymn to the eucharist, one that we hope will prove helpful in preparing for the sacrament and meditating on its grace.

—Barbara Ann Budde
J. Robert Baker

N ow on that same day two of them were going to a village called Emmaus, about seven miles from Jerusalem, and talking with each other about all these things that had happened. While they were talking and discussing, Jesus himself came near and went with them, but their eyes were kept from recognizing him. And he said to them, "What are you discussing with each other while you walk along?" They stood still, looking sad. Then one of them, whose name was Cleopas, answered him, "Are you the only stranger in Jerusalem who does not know the things that have taken place there in these days?" He asked them, "What things?" They replied "The things about Jesus of Nazareth, who was a prophet mighty in deed and word before God and all the people, and how our chief priests and leaders handed him over to be condemned to death and crucified him. But we had hoped that he was the one to redeem Israel. Yes, and besides all this, it is now the third day since these things took place. Moreover, some women of our group astounded us. They were at the tomb early this morning, and when they did not find his body there, they came back and told us that they had indeed seen a vision of angels who said that he was alive. Some of those who were with us went to the tomb and found it just as the women had said: but they did not see him." Then he said to them, "Oh, how foolish you are, and slow of heart to believe all that the prophets have declared! Was it not necessary that the Messiah should suffer these things and then enter into glory?" Then beginning with Moses and all the prophets, he interpreted to them the things about himself in all the scriptures.

As they came near the village to which they were going, he walked ahead as if he were going on. But they urged him strongly, saying, "Stay with us, because it is almost evening and the day is now nearly over." So he went in to stay with them. When he was at the table with them, he took bread, blessed and broke it, and gave it to them. Then their eyes were opened, and they recognized him: and he vanished from their sight. They said to each other, "Were not our hearts burning within us while he was talking to us on the road, while he was opening the scriptures to us?" That same hour they got up and returned to Jerusalem; and they found the eleven and their companions gathered together. They were saying, "The Lord has risen indeed, and he has appeared to Simon!" Then they told what had happened on the road, and how he had been made known to them in the breaking of the bread.

☐

LUKE 24:13–35

THEY SAID TO EACH OTHER, "WERE NOT OUR HEARTS BURNING
WITHIN US WHILE HE WAS TALKING TO US ON THE ROAD, WHILE
HE WAS OPENING THE SCRIPTURES TO US?"   Luke 24:32

~

PLEASE, sir, I want some more.

Charles Dickens
Nineteenth century

GOD of our fathers, I lie down without food,
I lie down hungry,
Although others have eaten and lie down full.
Even if it be but a polecat, or a little rock rabbit,
Give me and I shall be grateful!
I cry to God, Father of my ancestors.

Baralong tribe
South Africa

I am thirsty.

John 19:28b

AH, sir, God you save, and master mine!
A drink fain would I have, and somewhat to dine.

Miracle play
Fifteenth century

ONCE when Jacob was cooking a stew, Esau came in from the field, and he was famished. Esau said to Jacob, "Let me eat some of that red stuff, for I am famished!" (Therefore he was called Edom.) Jacob said, "First sell me your birthright." Esau said, "I am about to die; of what use is a birthright to me?" Jacob said, "Swear to me first." So he swore to him, and sold his birthright to Jacob. Then Jacob gave Esau bread and lentil stew, and he ate and drank, and rose and went his way.

Genesis 25:29–34

OUR bodily needs are real and important, and meeting them is as important as meeting any need of a whole, integrated personality. Feeding a hungry stomach is in no way less honorable than thinking lofty spiritual thoughts. But when we invest too much in feeding ourselves, and want too much in return, something goes wrong.

Doris Janzen Longacre
Twentieth century

DURING a period when the cost of living was very high, Rabbi Mendel noticed that the many needy people whom he entertained as guests in his house received smaller loaves than usual. He gave orders to make the loaves larger than before, since loaves were intended to adjust to hunger and not to the price.

Tales of the Hasidim
Eighteenth century

THERE was famine in every country, but throughout the land of Egypt there was bread. When all the land of Egypt was famished, the people cried to Pharaoh for bread. Pharaoh said to all the Egyptians, "Go to Joseph; what he says to you, do." And since the famine had spread over all the land, Joseph opened all the storehouses, and sold to the Egyptians, for the famine was severe in the land of Egypt. Moreover, all the world came to Joseph in Egypt to buy grain, because the famine became severe throughout the world.   Genesis 41:54–57

WE cannot think about feeding without also thinking about all those around the world and in our cities   Elizabeth Dodson Gray
who are dying from hunger and malnutrition.   Twentieth century

I have eaten too much, Lord,
While at that moment, in my town, more than fifteen
      hundred persons queued up at the breadline,
While in her attic a woman ate what she had salvaged that
      morning from the garbage cans.
While urchins in their tenement divided some scraps from
      the old folks' home,
While ten, a hundred, a thousand unfortunates throughout
      the world at that very moment twisted in pain and   Michael Quoist
      died of hunger before their despairing families.   Twentieth century

THEY wander abroad for bread,
saying, "Where is it?"
They know that a day of
darkness is ready at hand;
distress and anguish terrify them.

Job 15:23–24a

THE hungry sheep look up, and are not fed.

John Milton
Seventeenth century

THE rat deserts a room that is bare,
But Want, a cruel rat gnawing there,
Ate to the heart, all else was gone,
Nothing remained but Want alone.

Edith Sitwell
Twentieth century

In those days when there was again a great crowd without anything to eat, he called his disciples and said to them, "I have compassion for the crowd, because they have been with me now for three days and have nothing to eat. If I send them away hungry to their homes, they will faint on the way—and some of them have come from a great distance." His disciples replied, "How can one feed these people with bread here in the desert?" He asked them, "How many loaves do you have?" They said, "Seven." Then he ordered the crowd to sit down on the ground; and he took the seven loaves, and after giving thanks he broke them and gave them to his disciples to distribute; and they distributed them to the crowd. They had also a few small fish; and after blessing them, he ordered that these too should be distributed. They ate and were filled; and they took up the broken pieces left over, seven baskets full. Now there were about four thousand people. And he sent them away.

Mark 8:1–9

L ET us sit down soon to eat
with all those who haven't eaten,
let us spread great tablecloths,
put salt in the lakes of the world,
set up planetary bakeries,
tables with strawberries in snow,
and a plate like the moon itself
from which we will all eat.

For now I ask no more
than the justice of eating.

Pablo Neruda
Twentieth century

W HAT lies on the table is not wheat and grapes but
bread and wine, items created by fermentation and
fire, by processes of creative destruction instigated by human
agents for human purposes. What lies on the table is culture,
not nature. What lies there is fragrant with the musky pun-
gency of human intervention.

Nathan D. Mitchell
Twentieth century

H ERE, then, let the hungry Christ be fed; let the thirsty
Christ be given a drink; let the naked Christ be clothed;
let the stranger Christ be sheltered; let the sick Christ be
visited.

Augustine of Hippo
Fourth century

W E may not have people hungry for a plate of rice or for a piece of bread in New York City, but there is a tremendous hunger and a tremendous feeling of unwantedness everywhere. And that is really a very great poverty.
    We don't expect hunger here today, in Western countries. We don't expect, maybe, that terrible loneliness.
    But everywhere today hunger is not only for a piece of bread, but hunger for God, hunger for love.

Teresa of Calcutta
Twentieth century

I don't partake because I'm a good Catholic, holy and pious and sleek. I partake because I'm a bad Catholic, riddled by doubt and anxiety and anger: fainting from severe hypoglycemia of the soul. I need food.

Nancy Mairs
Twentieth century

I T seems to me that our three basic needs, for food and security and love, are so mixed and mingled and entwined that we cannot straightly think of one without the others. So it happens that when I write of hunger, I am really writing about love and the hunger for it, and warmth and the love of it and the hunger for it . . . and then the warmth and richness and fine reality of hunger satisfied . . . and it is all one.

M. F. K. Fisher
Twentieth century

B LESSED are you who are hungry now,
for you will be filled.

Luke 6:21

W HERE is the blessedness bestowed
On all that hunger after thee?
I hunger now, I thirst for God!
    See the poor fainting sinner, see,
And satisfy with endless peace,
And fill me with thy righteousness.

Charles Wesley
Eighteenth century

I hunger and I thirst:
    Jesu, my manna be;
Ye living waters, burst
    Out of the rock for me.

Thou bruised and broken Bread,
    My life-long wants supply;
As living souls are fed,
    O feed me, or I die.

Thou true life-giving Vine,
    Let me thy sweetness prove;
Renew my life with thine,
    Refresh my soul with love.

John S. B. Monsell
Nineteenth century

As a deer craves running water,
I thirst for you, my God;
I thirst for God,
the living God.

Psalm 42:2–3

For truly harts in the desert devour many reptiles and when their venom burns them, they try to come to the springs, to drink so as to assuage the venom's burning. It is the same for the monks: sitting in the desert they are burned by the venom of evil demons, and they long for Saturday and Sunday to come to be able to go to the springs of water, that is to say, the body and blood of the Lord, so as to be purified from the bitterness of the evil one.

Sayings of the Desert Fathers

When Helena, queen of Adiabene, entered the tomb which was the scene of the Resurrection she kissed the stone which the angel had rolled away from the door of the sepulchre. Indeed so ardent was her faith that she even licked with her mouth the very spot on which the Lord's body had lain, like one athirst for the river which he has longed for.

Jerome
Fourth century

We hunger and thirst after God. It is not enough for us to know him and to love him. We would clasp him, draw him to ourselves, hold him fast, and, bold as it sounds, we would take him into ourselves as we do our necessary food and drink, and thereby still and satisfy our hunger to the full.

Romano Guardini
Twentieth century

I yearn to see thee alone.
O God, I am neither anxious for home,
  nor for the forest of life;
I only yearn to see thee.
Yea I seek for nought save thee, O God,
  I yearn for thy vision alone; grant my prayer.

Dadu
Sixteenth century

M Y heart yearns for thee with a yearning which is never
stilled. Thou art my most precious possession, greater
and grander, lovelier and dearer by far than the life of my
body and the life of my spirit. My joy is in thee, my refuge
is in thee, my peace is in thee. Let me live before thee and
with thee and in thy sight, I humbly pray.

Zoroastrian prayer

H ARK ho! O ye hungry, ye thirsty and ragged,
I am the true bread, and the water of life —
Come here O ye filthy, ye crooked and cragged,
And ye shall be cleansed and quell'd from your strife.
Behold the bright Temple my God is erecting,
A mansion for those who are filthy and poor;
Its partments by Wisdom are now fast perfecting,
Come enter ye needy, but I am the door.

Shaker hymn

THE Ark of the Covenant becomes the Tabernacle, the Tent of Witness in the wilderness. But it rises higher still, and when the Israelites actually settle in Jerusalem, it becomes the Temple. What began as a threatening, aweful box of laws, becomes a lovely, graceful thing, the object of a centuries-long romance: "O how amiable are thy dwellings, thou Lord of hosts! My soul hath a desire and longing to enter into the courts of the Lord; my heart and my flesh rejoice in the living God."

Robert Farrar Capon
Twentieth century

HIS strength it is thy gates doth surely bar;
His grace in thee thy children multiplies;
By him thy borders lie secure from wars,
   And finest flour thy hunger satisfies.

Mary Herbert
Sixteenth century

Karl Rahner
Twentieth century

LET the infinite longing take power in us!

O Creator mine! Thou hast created my heart for thyself alone, and not for another, therefore this my heart can find no rest or ease save in thee; in thee who hast both created it and set in it this very longing for rest. Take away then from my heart all that is opposed to thee, and enter and abide and rule for ever. Amen.

Sadhu Sundar Singh
Twentieth century

O NE day—it was the 24th of March to be exact—I felt a very urgent wish to make my communion the next day—that is, on the Feast of the Annunciation of our Lady. I asked whether the church was far away, and was told it was about twenty miles. So I walked for the rest of that day and all the next night in order to get there in time for Matins. The weather was as bad as it could be, it snowed and rained, there was a strong wind and it was very cold. On my way I had to cross a small stream, and just as I got to the middle the ice gave way under my feet and I was plunged into the water up to my waist. Drenched like this, I came to Matins and stood through it, and also through the liturgy which fol-   *The Way of a Pilgrim* lowed, and at which by God's grace I made my communion.   Nineteenth century

T HEY are at rest in fulness of desire
    For what is given, they do not tire
Of the smart of the sun, the pleasant water-douse

    And riddled pool below,
Reproving our disgust and our ennui
    With humble insatiety.
Francis, perhaps, who lay in sister snow

    Before the wealthy gate
Freezing and praising, might have seen in this
    No trifle, but a shade of bliss—
That land of tolerable flowers, that state

    As near and far as grass
Where eyes become the sunlight, and the hand
    Is worthy of water: the dreamt land   Richard Wilbur
Toward which all hungers leap, all pleasures pass.   Twentieth century

THE Lord is my shepherd,
I need nothing more.
You gave me rest in green meadows,
setting me near calm waters,
where you revive my spirit.

You guide me along sure paths,
you are true to your name.
Though I should walk in death's dark valley,
I fear no evil with you by my side,
your shepherd's staff to comfort me.

You spread a table before me
as my foes look on.
You soothe my head with oil;
my cup is more than full.

Goodness and love wil tend me
every day of my life.
I will dwell in the house of the Lord
as long as I shall live.

Psalm 23

NOW ON THAT SAME DAY TWO OF THEM WERE GOING TO A VIL-
LAGE CALLED EMMAUS, ABOUT SEVEN MILES FROM JERUSALEM,
AND TALKING WITH EACH OTHER ABOUT ALL THESE THINGS THAT
HAD HAPPENED.   Luke 24:13–14

~

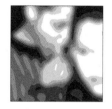

H APPENS like this. Feast gets talked up. Everyone hears about it, starts gettin' somethin' ready. Hunters hunt, bring fresh meat, people go fishin', bake bannock, everywhere there's people gettin' ready. That's the first sly part. Gettin' ready. Everyone wants to make up their best. Best moose stew, best bannock, best deer roast. Right away they're thinkin' of somethin' outside themselves. Thinkin' of the people. That's what our way's all about. Thinkin' of the people. Right away that simple ceremony's workin' on their thinkin'.

Then the gatherin' happens. People come together. See each other headin' together reminds 'em of how important they are to each other. Maybe how much they miss someone they ain't talked with for long time. Gets that feelin' movin' inside 'em.

Richard Wagamese
Twentieth century

W HAT is this place where we are meeting? Only a house, the earth its floor, Walls and a roof sheltering people, Windows for light, an open door. Yet it becomes a body that lives When we are gathered here, And know our God is near.

Huub Oosterhuis
Twentieth century

IN the windows you may see no light,
At the doors there may be no crowding,
In the voices heard no hint of Him,
No sound of The Name.
But He will come to the house
Through a thousand earth-fed fires,
Crashing a thousand chains.
He will find His way to the city,
And the streets will be bright with His Face,
And the lands loud with His Voice.
Then sleep will not break again or breath tear,
Or the multitudes mourn from room to room,
From tower to tower of flags aflame or falling.
He will come,
And within the eyes of the lonely women
By shaken pillars and shattered walls
Their souls will speak:
"Now does our sorrow seem old
For He is here and the enemy near no longer."

Francis J. O'Malley
Twentieth century

I had been hungry, all the Years—
My Noon had Come—to dine—
I trembling drew the Table near—
And touched the Curious Wine—

'Twas this on Tables I had seen—
When turning, hungry, Home
I looked in Windows, for the Wealth
I could not hope—for Mine—

I did not know the ample Bread—
'Twas so unlike the Crumb
The Birds and I, had often shared
In Nature's—Dining Room—

The Plenty hurt me—'twas so new—
Myself felt ill—and odd—
As Berry—of a Mountain Bush—
Transplanted—to the Road—

Nor was I hungry—so I found
That Hunger—was a way
Of Persons outside Windows—
The Entering—takes away—

Emily Dickinson
Nineteenth century

THE bread is broken and the wine poured out so that all of us separate persons can share and become one like the loaf and cup that were previously whole, one in Christ, like the christened loaf and the christened cup. In the breaking and the pouring, all the anguish of human contingency and limits and separateness and division. In the sharing, all the covenanted hope of freedom and fulfillment for the person and the person's love and unity and peace and communion with others, the making of the church.

Robert W. Hovda
Twentieth century

THERE'S no room for grace or gratitude in a world where reciprocal and observable relations are taken as the whole of what's meaningful and where we think we have total control. Nor is there any place for sin in a positive self-image permitting only good feelings.

Peggy Rosenthal
Twentieth century

HO, everyone who thirsts,
come to the waters;
and you that have no money,
  come, buy and eat!
Come, buy wine and milk
without money and without price.

Isaiah 55:1

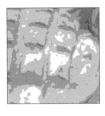

HE said also to the one who had invited him, "When you give a luncheon or a dinner, do not invite your friends or your brothers or your relatives or rich neighbors, in case they may invite you in return, and you would be repaid. But when you give a banquet, invite the poor, the crippled, the lame, and the blind. And you will be blessed, because they cannot repay you, for you will be repaid at the resurrection of the righteous."

Luke 14:12–14

THE banquet is ready the table is spread
And all who are willing may come and be fed
The Lord in his mercy hath open'd the door
His servants are calling the rich and the poor
The soul that is needy may come and secure
The riches of heaven a robe that is pure
With glory and comfort the feast doth abound
No lack of one blessing hath ever been found.

Shaker hymn

IT cannot be a matter of indifference to us who else is
invited to this wedding feast. Here you must greet your
neighbor and say, as it were: "How wonderful that you too
have been invited to his holy table and that we may eat this
holy food together!"

Balthasar Fischer
Twentieth century

As baptized Christians, we are really and truly brothers
and sisters in Jesus Christ, and when we receive the
holy eucharist this union is most perfectly reached, for then
we not only receive the King of Kings — in him we receive
each other.

Now there is no doubt that many people are not very keen
about receiving each other. They have a little complex that
revolts against the incorrect grammar their laundress uses,
the taste in hats of the woman three pews ahead. They have
a regular Great Wall of China of their own — enclosing themselves and acquaintances of similar tastes and capacities.

Mary Fabyan Windeatt
Twentieth century

THERE is not one of us, individually, racially, socially, who is fully complete in the sense of having in himself *all* the excellence of all humanity. And this excellence, this totality, is built up out of the contributions of the particular parts of it that we all can share with one another. I am therefore not completely human until I have found myself in my African and Asian and Indonesian brother because he has the part of humanity which I lack.

Thomas Merton
Twentieth century

UNEQUAL in degree, alike in size,
We make our flight, ascending toward the skies
And rise with those who by our help can rise.

Richard Wilbur
Twentieth century

SHE saw the streak as a vast swinging bridge extending upward from the earth through a field of living fire. Upon it a vast horde of souls were rumbling toward heaven. There were whole companies of white-trash, clean for the first time in their lives, and bands of black niggers in white robes, and battalions of freaks and lunatics shouting and clapping and leaping like frogs. And bringing up the end of the procession was a tribe of people whom she recognized at once as those who, like herself and Claud, had always had a little of everything and the God-given wit to use it right. She leaned forward to observe them closer. They were marching behind the others with great dignity, accountable as they had always been for good order and common sense and respectable behavior. They alone were on key. Yet she could see by their shocked and altered faces that even their virtues were being burned away.

Flannery O'Connor
Twentieth century

THE eucharistic table presents itself as the one place in our society where at least this much of God's kingdom is anticipated: where everyone is welcome, where those who are elsewhere unwelcome, outcasts, despised, oppressed, shunned, excluded are the most welcome of all.

Robert W. Hovda
Twentieth century

THROUGH this bread there comes about what we see in the gospel: a fellowship of pilgrims, a fellowship gathered around the apostles, a fellowship of a meal that includes everyone, a fellowship of one single pilgrim path to God.

Karl Rahner
Twentieth century

LET Mother Ecclesia
sing for joy!
Her children are found,
she gathers them home
to celestial harmony.
But you, vile serpent,
lie low! For those
your jealousy held in its maw
now shine in the blood of Christ.
Praise to our King,
praise to the Highest!
Alleluia.

Hildegard of Bingen
Twelfth century

I saw the throng, so deeply separate,
    Fed at one only board —
The devout people, moved, intent, elate,
    And the devoted Lord.

Oh struck apart! not side from human side,
    But soul from human soul,
As each asunder absorbed the multiplied,
    The ever unparted whole.

I saw this people as a field of flowers,
    Each grown at such a price
The sum of unimaginable powers
    Did no more than suffice.

A thousand single central daisies they,
    A thousand of the one;
For each, the entire monopoly of day;
    For each, the whole of the devoted sun.

Alice Meynell
Twentieth century

IN one fresco
the luminous
center
    a piece of bread

The Lord of His
    own Last Supper
holds to the mouth
    of its inseparable Guest,

All who eat there
    inseparable.

Louis Zukofsky
Twentieth century

Food, like sex, unites all creatures at the levels of both need and pleasure. But the sharing of food, like friendship itself, is potentially a more inclusive phenomenon than sex, for food can be shared with any other and with all others. As we have noted, Jesus' table fellowship with the outcasts of society, his eating with them as a friend, epitomized the scandal of inclusiveness for his time, for he invited the others that were rejected to the fellowship of a meal. Moreover, this table fellowship became both a symbol of the messianic banquet, where all would feast together in joy, and a precursor of the sacrament of the eucharist. Thus, Jesus' invitation to the outsiders to join him as friends at the table became an enacted parable of God's friendship with humanity: the God of Jesus is the One who invites us to table to eat together as friends.

Sallie McFague
Twentieth century

The Romans, Sossius Senecio, are fond of quoting a witty and sociable person who said, after a solitary meal, "I have eaten, but not dined today," implying that a "dinner" always requires friendly sociability for seasoning. Now Evenus said that a fire is the finest of seasonings; Homer calls salt "divine," and a colloquial term for salt is "graces," because when mixed with foods it will render most of them harmonious and agreeable and so "gracious" to our taste. But the most truly godlike seasoning at the dining-table is the presence of a friend or companion or intimate acquaintance — not because of his eating and drinking with us, but because he participates in the give-and-take of conversation, at least if there is something profitable and probable and relevant in what is said.

Plutarch
First century

WHEN the sun was about to set I looked and I saw a loaf of bread and a jar of water. He said to me, "Rise, my brother; eat and drink this little bit of water, for I see that you are exhausted from hunger and thirst and the hardships of the journey." I said to him, "As God Almighty lives, I will neither eat nor drink unless we sit down and eat together." Now when I continued to entreat him, he reluctantly agreed and so we sat down together. We divided the bread and ate and put some of it back; the two of us also drank from the jar of water and were satisfied and left some of the water in the jar. And we spent the whole night praying to God until morning.

Paphnutius
Fourth century

IF in other matters we are to preserve equality among people, why not begin with this first and accustom them to take their places with each other without vanity and ostentation, because they understand as soon as they enter the door that the dinner is a democratic affair and has no outstanding place like an acropolis where the rich are to recline and lord it over meaner folk?

Plutarch
First century

NOW all the tax collectors and sinners were coming near to listen to him. And the Pharisees and the scribes were grumbling and saying, "This fellow welcomes sinners and eats with them."

Luke 15:1–2

H E, upon whom the cherubim and seraphim dare not look in heaven, has sat down and eaten and drunk with tax collectors and sinners, out of his love, during the time he appeared on earth and went around amongst us in human body.

Pelagia
Fifth century

F OR God would make himself
Wholly like them,
And he would come to them
And dwell with them;

And God would be man
And man would be God,
And he would talk with them
And eat and drink with them;

And he himself would be
With them continually
Until the consummation
Of this world.

John of the Cross
Sixteenth century

A s Babette's red-haired familiar opened the door to the dining room, and the guests slowly crossed the threshold, they let go one another's hands and became silent. But the silence was sweet, for in spirit they still held hands and were still singing.

Babette had set a row of candles down the middle of the table; the small flames shone on the black coats and frocks and on the one scarlet uniform, and were reflected in clear, moist eyes.

Isak Dinesen
Twentieth century

WHEREIN lies happiness? In that which becks
Our ready minds to fellowship divine,
A fellowship with essence; till we shine,
Full alchemiz'd, and free of space. Behold
The clear religion of heaven!

John Keats
Nineteenth century

NEXT to her, holding lilies and a bottle of Poire William,
was a prematurely bald young man with a dark, with-
drawn face that was instantly familiar. "Where're your
things?" Egon said, making to go downstairs for the luggage. "We came as we were," said Toni, dumping her burden and hugging him, laughing.

Food, drink, and flowers lay on the old ottoman. That was to
be Toni's luggage, in future.

Nadine Gordimer
Twentieth century

COME together on the Lord's day,
break bread and give thanks,
having first confessed your sins
so that your sacrifice may be pure.
Anyone who has a quarrel with his fellow
should not gather with you
until he has been reconciled,
lest your sacrifice be profaned.

For this is the sacrifice of which the Lord says:
"In every place and at every time
offer me a pure sacrifice,
for I am a great king, says the Lord,
and my name is marvelous among the nations."

Didache
Second century

O lead my blindness by the hand,
Lead me to thy familiar feast,
Not here or now to understand,
  Yet even here and now to taste,
How the eternal Word of heaven
On earth in broken bread is given.

William Ewart
Gladstone
Nineteenth century

THE Lord appeared to Abraham by the oaks of Mamre, as he sat at the entrance of his tent in the heat of the day. He looked up and saw three men standing near him. When he saw them, he ran from the tent entrance to meet them, and bowed down to the ground. He said, "My lord, if I find favor with you, do not pass by your servant. Let a little water be brought, and wash your feet, and rest yourselves under the tree. Let me bring a little bread, that you may refresh yourselves, and after that you may pass on — since you have come to your servant." So they said, "Do as you have said." And Abraham hastened into the tent to Sarah, and said, "Make ready quickly three measures of choice flour, knead it, and make cakes." Abraham ran to the herd, and took a calf, tender and good, and gave it to the servant, who hastened to prepare it. Then he took curds and milk and the calf that he had prepared, and set it before them; and he stood by them under the tree while they ate.

Genesis 18:1 – 8

Do you know the difference between our Father Abraham, peace be with him, and Lot? Why does such a spirit of satisfaction pervade the story of how Abraham set before the angels curd and milk and tender calf? Did not Lot also bake for them and give them to eat? And why is the fact that Abraham received them in his tent regarded as so deserving an action? For Lot also asked them in and gave them shelter. Now this is the truth of the matter: In the case of Lot it is written that angels came to Sodom. But concerning Abraham, the Scriptures say: ". . . and he lifted up his eyes and looked, and lo, three men stood over against him." Lot saw angelic shapes, Abraham poor, dusty wayfarers in need of food and rest.

Levi Yitzhak of
Berditchev
Eighteenth century

Abba Pseleusius also said: "When, therefore, I had come to him — that is, to John about whom I first spoke and about whom I have said these things — he received me with great hospitality. I found nothing in his dwelling except three loaves of bread, and they were there only for strangers who should pass by, so it would not be said, "The old man does not eat bread."

Paphnutius
Fourth century

A LKÍNOÖS, this will not pass for courtesy:
a guest abased in ashes at our hearth?
Everyone here awaits your word; so come, then,
lift the man up; give him a seat of honor,
a silver-studded chair. Then tell the stewards
we'll have another wine bowl for libation.

Homer
Ninth century BCE

L OVE bade we welcome: yet my soul drew back,
Guiltie of dust and sinne.
But quick-ey'd Love, observing me grow slack
From my first entrance in,
Drew nearer to me, sweetly questioning,
If I lack'd any thing.

A guest, I answer'd, worthy to be here:
Love said, You shall be he.
I the unkinde, ungratefull? Ah my deare,
I cannot look on thee.
Love took my hand, and smiling did reply,
Who made the eyes but I?

Truth Lord, but I have marr'd them: let my shame
Go where it doth deserve.
And know you not, sayes Love, who bore the blame?
My deare, then I will serve.
You must sit down, sayes Love, and taste my meat:
So I did sit and eat.

George Herbert
Seventeenth century

WASHED into the doorway
by the wake of the traffic,
he wears humanity
like a third-hand shirt
—blackened with enough
of Manhattan's dirt to sprout
a tree, or poison one.
His empty hand has led him
where he has come to.
Our differences claim us.
He holds out his hand,
in need of all that's mine.

And so we're joined, as deep
as son and father. His life
is offered me to choose.

Wendell Berry
Twentieth century

W E, this community, this body of Christ, are the mystery of the Son of God in the midst of the world. We see the Spirit of God not in some puff of cloud hovering near the sun in the sky; we see that Spirit in the eyes and palms and lips of the faithful who come forward to eat and to drink. In the bread is the body of the Son, in the eating of the bread is the Spirit of God.

Gail Ramshaw
Twentieth century

T HE community was a source of the presence of the Lord. The community was called to be and to become the holy communion that was to be world transforming.

Shawn Madigan
Twentieth century

T HIS was a real nice clambake,
We're mighty glad we came,
The vittles we et were good, you bet!
The company was the same,
Our hearts are warm, our bellies are full
and we are feelin' prime.
This was a real nice clambake
and we all had a real good time!

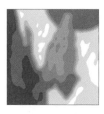

Oscar Hammerstein II
Twentieth century

WHILE THEY WERE TALKING AND DISCUSSING, JESUS HIMSELF

CAME NEAR AND WENT WITH THEM.   Luke 24:15

~

B EFORE the food comes one of the elders'll get up'n say *a* big prayer. Big long prayer. Me I remember one time that old woman who was prayin' prayed so long I kinda fell asleep. It was all the rustlin' around woke me up. Gladda that. Never wanna miss no feast. Heh, heh, heh. Anyway, the elders, men or women, they pray and give thanks for the food, the land, the people, the gatherin', everythin'. That's another sly part. Big reminder of where it all comes from. Everythin'. Hunters remember that it wasn't them that brought the deer, wasn't fishermen brought the fish. It all came from the Creator. That's what that prayer tells 'em.

Richard Wagamese
Twentieth century

T O God belongs the praise, Lord of the heavens and Lord of the earth, the Lord of all being. His is the dominion in the heavens and in the earth: He is the Almighty, the ever-wise.

Qur'an

Holy is God, the Father of all,
Holy is God, whose will is accomplished
   by his own powers,
Holy is God, who wills to be known
   and is known by his own,
Holy art thou, who by Logos has constituted
   all existing things,
Holy art thou, of whom all nature was born as the image,
Holy art thou, whom nature has not formed,
Holy art thou, who art more mighty than all power,
Holy art thou, who art greater than all eminence,
Holy art thou, who art superior to all praises.

Hermetic Corpus
First to third centuries

GREAT is, O King, our happiness
in thy kingdom, thou, our King.

We dance before thee, Our King,
By the strength of thy kingdom.

May our feet be made strong;
Let us dance before thee, eternal.

Give you praise, all angels,
To him above who is worthy of praise.

Zulu Nazarite prayer

SMALL it is, in this poor sort
To enrol thee:
E'en eternitie's too short
   To extol thee.

George Herbert
Seventeenth century

ALL you big things, bless the Lord
Mount Kilimanjaro and Lake Victoria
The Rift Valley and the Serengeti Plain
Fat baobabs and shady mango trees
All eucalyptus and tamarind trees
Bless the Lord
Praise and extol him for ever and ever.

All you tiny things, bless the Lord
Busy black ants and hopping fleas
Wriggling tadpoles and mosquito larvae
Flying locusts and water drops
Pollen dust and tsetse flies
Millet seeds and dried dagaa
Bless the Lord
African canticle   Praise and extol him for ever and ever.

THE ancient Israelites offered animals or food to God to praise God and to thank God for blessings received. The reason food or animal sacrifice was offered to God (or the gods) was that these things were central to the life of the people. In this way, the sacrifice was seen as a sharing of one's life with God.

William A. Anderson
Twentieth century

AT the last supper,
as he sat at table with his apostles,
he offered himself to you as the spotless lamb,
Roman Missal   the acceptable gift that gives you perfect praise.

W<small>E</small> have our victim in heaven, our priest in heaven, our sacrifice in heaven. Let us then present such sacrifices as can be offered on that altar, no longer sheep and oxen, no longer blood and steaming fat. All these things have been done away, and in their place the reasonable service has been brought in.

John Chrysostom
Fourth century

T<small>HE</small> purpose of celebrating the liturgy is not to give lip-service to God, but to glorify him as Jesus glorified him. We do this by transforming our lives under the influence of the Spirit of Jesus so that we become increasingly Christ-like in our total devotion to God and to the welfare of others. Jesus glorified his Father before the world by being totally given over to the Father's work in the world, no matter what the cost to himself. We celebrate the memory of Jesus in the Eucharistic sacrifice by offering our own lives together with Jesus for the life of the world.

Mark Searle
Twentieth century

I<small>T</small> is in public prayer that we learn to pray — or discover to our sorrow that we cannot pray. Thus we may and must also ask of our prayer what style of life it forms. Are our prayers diffuse and amorphous and so incapable of forming a coherent way of life? Do they turn our attention upon ourselves or toward the One who delivers us from bondage to ourselves? Do they summon us to anxiety and busyness or do they cry out for God, the God who promises to come to us and has come to us in the cross and resurrection of Jesus? Do the prayers we pray summon us to the illusions of self-congratulation and ephemeral piety, or do they unmask our aching, our yearning, our call to God? Do the prayers we pray join us in solidarity with the groaning of our sisters and brothers and the whole of creation, or do they leave us finally alone in the echo chamber of our self-preoccupation? All of these questions are finally only one question: Do we know what it is to pray for the reign of God, on earth as in heaven, in the name of Jesus who cried out for God upon his cross?

Theodore W. Jennings, Jr.
Twentieth century

SINCE once again, Lord, as in another time in the forests along the Aisne, I have neither bread nor wine nor altar here on the Asian steppes, I lift myself far above symbols, to the pure majesty of the Real; and I, your priest, offer to you on the altar of the entire earth, the travail and suffering of the world. Yonder breaks the sun, to light the uttermost east, and then to send its sheets of fire over the living surface of the earth, which wakens, shudders, and resumes its appalling struggle.

Teilhard de Chardin
Twentieth century

DECK thyself, my soul, with gladness,
Leave the gloomy haunts of sadness;
Come into the daylight's splendour,
There with joy thy praises render
Unto him whose grace unbounded
Hath this wondrous banquet founded:
High o'er all the heavens he reigneth,
Yet to dwell with thee he deigneth.

Johann Franck
Nineteenth century

AT the Lamb's high feast we sing
Praise to our victorious King,
Who hath washed us in the tide
Flowing from his pierced side;
Praise we him, whose love divine
Gives his sacred Blood for wine,
Gives his Body for the feast,
Christ the Victim, Christ the Priest.

R. Campbell
Nineteenth century

THE poor eat and are satisfied; those who seek the Lord shall praise him, and their hearts shall live for ever.

Orthodox liturgy

WE praise you, God almighty,
who sit above the Cherubim
and above the Seraphim,
whom prophets and apostles praise!

We praise you, Lord, with our prayers,
you who came to free us from sin!
We pray you, exalted Redeemer,
whom the Father sent to shepherd the sheep:
You are Christ the Lord, the Savior,
born of the Virgin Mary.
Deliver forever from all sin
us who take this chalice most holy!

Anonymous
Fourth century

WHAT gift can ever repay
God's gift to me?
I raise the cup of freedom
as I call on God's name!
I fulfill my vows to you, Lord,
standing before your assembly.

Psalm 116:12–14

G ODHEAD here in hiding, whom I do adore
  Masked by these bare shadows,
      shape and nothing more,
See, Lord, at thy service low lies here a heart
Lost, all lost in wonder at the God thou art.

Anonymous
Thirteenth century

I have taken in the light
  that quickened eye and leaf.
May my brain be bright with praise
of what I eat, in the brief blaze
of motion and of thought.
May I be worthy of my meat.

Wendell Berry
Twentieth century

O Lord,
  you are the host and the meal;
you invite and you are the feast.
You invited us to share in this Passover
by giving us your body and blood.
May we share in your passion and death
so that we may one day be reborn with you in glory,
praising you for ever.

Maronite liturgy

YET the time will come
To the heart's dark slum
When the rich man's gold and the rich man's wheat
Will grow in the street, that the starved may eat—
And the sea of the rich will give up its dead—
And the last blood and fire from my side will be shed.   Edith Sitwell
For the fires of God go marching on.   Twentieth century

DRAW nigh and take the Body of the Lord,
And drink the holy Blood for you outpoured.

Saved by that Body and that holy Blood,   Latin hymn
With souls refreshed, we render thanks to God.   Seventh century

THE one word *thanks* slipped from Whit in a murmur, and
he sat near the back on the hardest pew he'd yet encoun-
tered in a lifetime of pews. All the other people knelt as
they entered and said silent prayers. . . . The sight, and the
slow transaction at the altar, held Whit so close he forgot the
woman he saw outside. . . . And only toward the end of the
service did his eyes drift rightward and catch the woman's
face again, the great dark fall of her lustrous hair. In the series
of sick wards Whit occupied, he often struggled at night for
reasons to live, awake, through one more day. And tonight
as he saw this woman, he thought *I wish I'd known this,
just this picture.*

Even as a child he cared a good deal for beautiful sights—
mostly trees and the arrowheads he found, a rare deer or
bird. He saved them up as other boys save baseball cards
or agate marbles to tide them over. And when he was old
enough to save the sight and smell of beautiful women, it
was not always as a goad for sex, sights to rub his body
against, but as frank reminders of the world's amazing ten-   Reynolds Price
dency to please.   Twentieth century

Richard Wilbur
Twentieth century

THERE, there is nothing else but grace and measure,
Richness, quietness, and pleasure.

Sayings of the
Desert Fathers

As he was dying, Abba Benjamin said to his sons, "If you observe the following, you can be saved, 'Be joyful at all times, pray without ceasing and give thanks for all things.' "

Didache
Second century

FIRST, for the cup:
"We thank you, our Father,
for the holy vine of David your servant
which you have revealed to us through Jesus your Child.
    Glory be yours through all ages!"

Cyril of Jerusalem
Fourth century

THEN, after sharing in the body of Christ, draw near also to the cup of his blood. Do not stretch out your hands, but bow in adoration and respect, and say: "Amen." Then sanctify yourself further by sharing in the blood of Christ. And while your lips are still wet, touch them with your fingers and sanctify your eyes, your forehead, and your other senses. Then, while waiting for the prayer, give thanks to God who has judged you worthy of such great mysteries.

DEAR MISS MANNERS:
What is the procedure when one has the first bite of potato halfway to the mouth and then discovers that everyone else is waiting for the host to say grace? Do you proceed and pop it into the mouth, or lay the fork down at once? If the former, does this invalidate the grace?

GENTLE READER:
God will forgive all sins, even gluttony, but to talk with your mouth full — even to say "Amen" — is unforgivable in this life. Therefore, Miss Manners considers it theologically safer to put down the fork, gracefully.

Judith Martin
Twentieth century

KING Melchizedek of Salem brought out bread and wine; he was priest of God Most High.

He blessed him and said,
"Blessed be Abram by God Most High,
    maker of heaven and earth;
and blessed be God Most High,
    who has delivered your enemies into your hand!"

Genesis 14:18–20

THE table awaits us at which our baptismal life is fed over and over again. We have every reason to cry out in gratitude: alleluia, alleluia!

Balthasar Fischer
Twentieth century

THE meal is ready: come and enjoy it.
    The calf is a fat one: you will not go hungry away.
There's kindness for all to partake of and kindness to spare.

Hippolytus of Rome
Second century

Dᴜʀɪɴɢ the last two years of his life, Rabbi Elimelekh ate and drank only very little, and even that little he took only because his family urged him to. Once, when his son Eleazar begged him with tears to eat at least enough to keep him alive, he said with a smile on his lips: "Oh, what coarse food you set before me! Now, if I could only get a plate of gruel, the kind my brother Zusya and I were served in the little red inn on the Dniester, in the days of our wanderings!"

Some time after Rabbi Elimelekh's death, his son set out on a journey to the little red inn on the Dniester. When he arrived there, he asked for a night's lodging and inquired what there was for supper. "We are poor people," said the innkeeper's wife. "We give the peasants vodka in exchange for flour and dried peas and beans. Most of this my husband takes to market and barters for more vodka, and the rest we eat. So I can offer you nothing but gruel for supper."

"Prepare it for me right away," said Rabbi Eleazar. By the time he had said the Evening Prayer, the soup was on the table. He ate one plate of it, and then another, and asked for a third helping. "Tell me what it was you put into the soup to make it so tasty?"

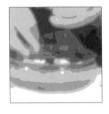

"Believe me, sir," she said. "I put nothing into it at all." But when he pressed her, she finally said: "Well, if it tastes so good to you, paradise itself is responsible for it." And now she told: "It is very long ago, but once two pious men stopped here. You could see that they were true zaddikim. And because I had nothing to serve them except gruel, I prayed to God while I was cooking it: "Lord of the world, I have nothing else in the house, and you have everything. So have mercy upon your tired and hungry servants and put some herbs from paradise into their soup!" And when the gruel was put on the table, the two of them emptied the whole big bowl, and I refilled it and they emptied it a second time, and one of them said to me: 'Daughter, your soup tastes of paradise.' And just now I prayed again."

Tales of the Hasidim
Eighteenth century

I N the sacrament of Christ's redemptive sacrifice, we also celebrate and consecrate our own gifts. We identify our lives, our labors, our passions, and our joys with the body, blood, history, and person of Jesus. It is an attempt to reconfirm our choice of loving and life-giving service, as we reproduce in ourselves not only the manner of Jesus' death and resurrection, but also the very substance of Jesus' reality as food for his brothers and sisters.

John Kavanaugh
Twentieth century

I N the Mass we have Jesus in the appearance of bread, while in the slums we see Christ and touch him in the broken bodies and in the abandoned children.

Teresa of Calcutta
Twentieth century

F OR you must know, beloved, that each one of us is beyond all question responsible for all men and all things on earth, not only because of the general transgressions of the world, but each one individually for all men and every single man on this earth. This realization is the crown of a monk's way of life, and, indeed, of every person on earth.

Fyodor Dostoyevsky
Nineteenth century

I N the days of his flesh, Jesus offered up prayers and supplications, with loud cries and tears, to the one who was able to save him from death, and he was heard because of his reverent submission. Although he was a Son, he learned obedience through what he suffered; and having been made perfect, he became the source of eternal salvation for all who obey him, having been designated by God a high priest according to the order of Melchizedek.

Hebrews 5:7–10

R ABBI Mendel's wife could not bring Rabbi Mendel, who was sitting over his books in the House of Study, a thing to eat for three days. On the third day she ventured to cross the baker's threshold one more time. He turned her away. Silently she left the shop. But he followed her and offered her bread and other food, as much as she could carry, if she on her part would promise him her share in the world to come. She hesitated only an instant. Then she accepted his offer.

When she entered the House of Study she saw her husband sitting in his seat. He was almost unconscious, but the book was gripped firmly in both his hands. She spread the cloth, served him, and watched him while he ate. He looked up, for never before had she remained. They looked at each other. When their eyes met, she saw he knew what she had done. And then she saw that at that moment she had received a new share in the coming world.

Tales of the Hasidim
Eighteenth century

W HO offers food, offers self. This is true of my giving a sandwich to a person at the door, or of my entertaining friends in the kitchen or the dining room. It is also true of banquets, where the servers are the ambassadors and representatives of the host who gives the food. It is true of farmers who raise food, of butchers who dress meats, of bakers who make bread, of grandmothers who put up preserves, of anyone who peels, cooks or prepares food for others. It is also true of every Christian who offers the bread and wine at the sacrifice of the Mass.

Adé Bethune
Twentieth century

A BBA Isaiah also said that when there was an agape and the brethren were eating in the church and talking to one another, the priest of Pelusiam reprimanded them in these words, "Brethren, be quiet. For I have seen a brother eating with you and drinking as many cups as you and his prayer is ascending to the presence of God like fire."

Sayings of the Desert Fathers

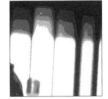

W HEN it was time to eat, St. Francis and St. Clare sat down together, and one of his companions with St. Clare's companion, and all his other companions were grouped around that humble table. But at the first course St. Francis began to speak about God in such a sweet and holy and profound and divine and marvelous way that he himself and St. Clare and her companion and all the others who were at that poor little table were rapt in God by the overabundance of divine grace that descended upon them.

And while they were sitting there, in a rapture, with their eyes and hands raised to heaven, it seemed to the people of Assisi and Bettona and the entire district that the Church of St. Mary of the Angels and the whole place and the forest which was at that time around the place were all aflame and that an immense fire was burning over all of them. Consequently the people of Assisi ran down there in great haste to save the place and put out the fire, as they firmly believed that everything was burning up.

But when they reached the place, they saw that nothing was on fire. Entering the place, they found St. Francis with St. Clare and all the companions sitting around that very humble table, rapt in God by contemplation and invested with power from on high.

The Little Flowers of St. Francis
Fourteenth century

To know too that you are in the Communion of Saints —
to know that you have cast your lot among all those
blessed servants of God who are the choice fruit of his
Passion — that you have their intercessions on high — that
you may address them — and above all the glorious Mother
of God, what thoughts can be greater than these? To know in
short that the atonement of Christ is not a thing at a distance,
or like the sun standing over against us and separated off
from us, but that we are surrounded by an atmosphere and
are in a medium, through which his warmth and light flow
in upon us on every side, what can one ask, what can one
desire, more than this?

John Henry Newman
Nineteenth century

LET us break bread together on our knees;
Let us break bread together on our knees;
   When I fall on my knees,
   With my face to the rising sun,
   O Lord, have mercy on me.

Let us drink wine together on our knees;
Let us drink wine together on our knees;
   When I fall on my knees,
   With my face to the rising sun,
   O Lord, have mercy on me.

Let us praise God together on our knees;
Let us praise God together on our knees;
   When I fall on my knees,
   With my face to the rising sun,
   O Lord, have mercy on me.

American folk hymn

BREAD-BREAKERS become bread broken; the diners become the world's dinner; the body *at* the table becomes the body *on* the table. For the life of the world.

Nathan D. Mitchell
Twentieth century

O salutaris hostia,
Quæ cæli pandis ostium:
Bella premunt hostilia,
Da robur fer auxilium.

Uni trinoque Domino
Sit sempiterna gloria:
Qui vitam sine termino
Nobis donet in patria.

O Saving Victim, opening wide
The gate of heaven to all below!
Our foes press on from every side:
Your aid supply, your strength bestow.

To your great name be endless praise,
Immortal Godhead, One in Three;
O grant us endless length of days
When our true native land we see.

Thomas Aquinas
Thirteenth century

THEN BEGINNING WITH MOSES AND ALL THE PROPHETS, HE
INTERPRETED TO THEM THE THINGS ABOUT HIMSELF IN ALL THE
SCRIPTURES.   Luke 24:27

~

O Wealth of the poor, how wonderfully can you sustain
souls, revealing your great riches to them gradually
and not permitting them to see them all at once! Since the
time of that vision I have never seen such great Majesty, hid-
den in a thing so small as the Host, without marvelling at
your great wisdom.

Teresa of Avila
Sixteenth century

THIS day shall be a day of remembrance for you. You shall
celebrate it as a festival to the Lord; throughout your
generations you shall observe it as a perpetual ordinance.
Seven days you shall eat unleavened bread; on the first day
you shall remove leaven from your houses, for whoever eats
leavened bread from the first day until the seventh day shall
be cut off from Israel.

Exodus 12:14–15

FATHER,
we now celebrate this memorial of our redemption.
We recall Christ's death, his descent among the dead,
his resurrection, and his ascension to your right hand;
and, looking forward to his coming glory,
we offer you his body and blood,
the acceptable sacrifice
which brings salvation to the whole world.

Roman Missal

W HAT he did at supper seated,
Christ ordained to be repeated,
His memorial ne'er to cease:

And his rule for guidance taking,
Bread and wine we hallow, making
Thus our sacrifice of peace.

Sequence for
Corpus Christi

T HE Eucharistic celebration is an act of remembering
before God the self-sacrifice of Jesus who, in submission
to his Father and for love of us all, did not try to evade
death, but let himself be crucified and killed rather than be
unfaithful.

Mark Searle
Twentieth century

D O you remember the good years in Canaan?
The summers were endlessly gold.
The fields were a patchwork of clover,
the winters were never too cold.
We strolled down the boulevard together,
and ev'rything round us was fine.

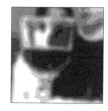

Do you remember those wonderful parties?
The splendour of Canaan's cuisine.
Our extravagant, elegant soirées,
the gayest the Bible has seen.

Tim Rice
Twentieth century

BUT what I remember most, and most gratefully, is Dick's own presence, for he was a man fully present in the place and its yearly round of work that connected hayfield and grainfield and feed barn and hog lot, woods and woodpile and the wood box behind the kitchen stove, well and drinking trough. When the work was to be done, he was there to do it. He did it well and without haste; when it was done he took his ease and did not complain. Years later, when I was looking for the way home, his was one of the minds that guided me.

Wendell Berry
Twentieth century

As human beings living together in a concerned society, we must have the ability to remember. Our whole life is shaped by our memories of our families, our friends, our memories of shared joys and tragedies, our recollections of birth and death.

William A. Anderson
Twentieth century

ACCORDING to thy gracious word,
In meek humility,
This will I do, my dying Lord,
I will remember Thee.

Thy body, broken for my sake,
My bread from heav'n shall be;
Thy testamental cup I take,
And thus remember thee.

James Montgomery
Nineteenth century

THE communities of memory . . . are concerned in a variety of ways to give a qualitative meaning to the living of life, to time and space, to persons and groups. Religious communities, for example, do not experience time in the way the mass media present it — as a continuous flow of qualitatively meaningless sensations. The day, the week, the season, the year are punctuated by an alternation of the sacred and the profane. Prayer breaks into our daily life at the beginning of a meal, at the end of the day, at common worship, reminding us that our utilitarian pursuits are not the whole of life, that a fulfilled life is one in which God and neighbor are remembered first. Many of our religious traditions recognize the significance of silence as a way of breaking the incessant flow of sensations and opening our hearts to the wholeness of being.

Robert Bellah, et al.
Twentieth century

WE have lost the simplest gratitude.
    We lack the knowledge we showed ten
thousand years past, that you live
a goddess but mortal, that what we take
must be returned; that the poison we drop
in you will stunt our children's growth.

Marge Piercy
Twentieth century

THE road was a little smoother, following streambeds under the live-oaks that grow in all the gentle creases of the dry tawny hills of that part of California. We came to a shack where there was water for sale, and a table under the dark wide trees.

Then we sat on a rough bench at the table, the three of us in the deep green twilight, and had one of the nicest suppers I have ever eaten.

The strange thing about it is that all three of us have told other people the same thing, without ever talking of it among ourselves until lately. Father says that all his nervousness went away, and he saw us for the first time as two little brown humans who were fun. Anne and I both felt a subtle excitement at being alone for the first time with the only man in the world we loved.

M. F. K. Fisher
Twentieth century

MY aunt often said that Myra was incorrigibly extravagant; but I saw that her chief extravagance was in caring for so many people and in caring for them so much. . . . Her voice invested the name with a sort of grace. . . . When she addressed Aunt Lydia, for instance, she seemed to be speaking to a person deeper down than the blurred, taken-for-granted image of my aunt that I saw every day, and for a moment my aunt became more individual, less matter-of-fact to me.

Willa Cather
Twentieth century

M Y heart, being hungry, feeds on food
The fat of heart despise.
Beauty where beauty never stood,
    And sweet where no sweet lies
I gather to my querulous need,
Having a growing heart to feed.

It may be, when my heart is dull,
    Having attained its girth,
I shall not find so beautiful
    The meagre shapes of earth,
Nor linger in the rain to mark
The smell of tansy through the dark.

Edna St. Vincent Millay
Twentieth century

T HE bread that feeds the heavens
is here on the altar:
the God who cannot die is killed,
is killed for sacrifice
in this mystery.
This food he gives brings life
to those who caught their death
from what was once their food in Eden.

The blood that streams from him he pours
into the chalice.
The priest of the new dispensation
makes it a sacred oblation;
the faithful take it
and wash themselves clean.

One with his Father,
now as of old,
he opens his heart
to the world.

Anonymous
Fourth or fifth century

I know exactly what 'Lamb of God' means," he said. "Each year at lambing time, there are lambs and ewes who do not make it. Inevitably, on one side of the field is a ewe whose lamb has died. The ewe is filled with milk but will not nourish any lamb she does not recognize as her own. Inevitably, on the other side of the field is a lamb whose mother has died. That lamb will starve because no ewe will accept and nourish it. So the shepherd takes the dead lamb and slits its throat, and pours its blood over the body of the living lamb. Recognizing the blood, the ewe will now nurse and save the orphaned lamb. Through the gift of the blood of the lamb who has died, the living lamb is recognized and restored to the fold, nourished, and saved. That is the Lamb of God."

Barbara Williamson
Twentieth century

DYING you destroyed our death.
Rising you restored our life.
Lord Jesus, come in glory

Roman Missal

As often as the commemoration of this victim is celebrated, so often is the work of our salvation being done.

Roman Missal

THE real starting point of the Christian mystery is not the memorial of a death but the recognition of an enduring life. . . . Indeed, it is the fact of the life which endorses the sacrificial and redemptive character of the death.

Evelyn Underhill
Twentieth century

THIS holy Mass, this eucharist is clearly an act of faith. Our Christian faith shows us that in this moment contention is changed into the body of the Lord who offers himself for the redemption of the world. In the chalice, the wine is transformed into the blood that was the price of salvation. This body broken and this blood shed for human beings encourage us to give our body and blood up to suffering and pain, as Christ did — not for self, but to bring justice and peace to our people.

Oscar Romero
Twentieth century

Flannery O'Connor
Twentieth century

IF it were only a symbol, I'd say to hell with it.

FOR this bread is in very truth the precious Body of our Lord and God, and Saviour, Jesus Christ.

For this chalice is, in very truth the precious Blood of our Lord and God, and Saviour, Jesus Christ, which was poured out for the life of the world, transmuting them by thy Holy Spirit.

Liturgy of Basil
the Great

C OME, O faithful ones,
    let us enjoy the Lord's hospitality,
the banquet of immortality.
In the upper chamber, with minds uplifted,
let us learn the Word from the Word
Orthodox liturgy   whom we magnify.

T HIS is the hour of banquet and of song;
    This is the heav'nly table spread for me;
Here let me feast and, feasting still prolong
The brief bright hour of fellowship with thee.

Feast after feast thus comes and passes by;
Yet, passing, points to the glad feast above,
Horatius Bonar   Giving sweet foretaste of the festal joy,
Nineteenth century   The lamb's great marriage feast of bliss and love.

A second meaning of "Do this in memory of me" is thus
    "Gather up all your fleshly memories of table—of food
and fun, tears and laughter, mellowness and mirth—for they
Nathan D. Mitchell   have become your own body. Your body is both *at* the table
Twentieth century   and *on* the table. You are looking at what you have become."

THEY shall come and sing aloud on the height of Zion,
and they shall be radiant over the goodness
   of the LORD,
over the grain, the wine, and the oil,
   and over the young of the flock and the herd;
their life shall become like a watered garden,
   and they shall never languish again.   Jeremiah 31:12

WE ate with steeps of sky about our shoulders,
High up a mountainside,
On a terrace like a raft roving
Seas of view.

The tablecloth was green, and blurred away
Toward verdure far and wide,
And all the country came to be
Our table too.

We drank in tilted glasses of rosé
From tinted peaks of snow,
Tasting the frothy mist, and freshest
Fathoms of air.

Richard Wilbur
Twentieth century

From blossoms
released
by the moonlight,
from an
aroma of exasperated
love,
steeped in fragrance,
yellowness
drifted from the lemon tree,
and from its planetarium
lemons descended to the earth.

Tender yield!
The coasts,
the markets glowed
with light, with
unrefined gold;
we opened
two halves
of a miracle,
congealed acid
trickled
from the hemispheres
of a star,
the most intense liqueur
of nature,
a unique, vivid,
concentrated,
born of the cool, fresh
lemon,
of its fragrant house,
its acid, secret symmetry.

Knives
slice a small
cathedral
in the lemon,
the concealed apse, opened,
revealed acid stained glass,
drops
oozed topaz
altars,
cool architecture.

So, when you hold
the hemisphere
of a cut lemon
above your plate
you spill
a universe of gold,
a
yellow goblet
of miracles,
a fragrant nipple
of the earth's breast,
a ray of light that was made fruit,
the minute fire of a planet.

Pablo Neruda
Twentieth century

Mechthild of Magdeburg
Thirteenth century

Y OUR noble desire and your insatiable hunger I shall satisfy eternally with my infinite superabundance.

F OR sometimes they call it *Eucharist,* which word we may
render either by *good grace,* or by *thanksgiving.* And
rightly, indeed, is it to be called *good grace,* as well because
it first signifies eternal life, concerning which it has been
written: *The grace of God is eternal life,* and also because it
contains Christ the Lord, who is true grace and the fountain
of all favors.

Catechism of the
Council of Trent

I 'VE just come from the fountain,
I've just come from the fountain,
Lord, I've just come from the fountain,
His name's so sweet.

O brothers, I love Jesus,
O brothers, I love Jesus,
O brothers, I love Jesus,
His name's so sweet.

O sisters, I love Jesus,
O sisters, I love Jesus,
O sisters, I love Jesus,
His name's so sweet.

Been drinking from the fountain,
Been drinking from the fountain,
Been drinking from the fountain,
His name's so sweet.

African American
spiritual

O<small>NLY</small> water—

We seek of the water
The water's love!

Shall we go again
Breast to water-breast,

Gather the fish-substance,
The shining fire,
the phosphor-subtlety?

We sing who were many in the South,
At each live river mouth
Sparse-lighted, carried along!

Louis Zukofsky
Twentieth century

T<small>HIS</small> feast of the Spirit
leads the mystic dance through the year.
The Pasch came from God, came from heaven to earth;
from earth it has gone back to heaven.
New is this feast and all-embracing;
all creation assembles at it.

Hippolytus of Rome
Second century

L ET us praise our Maker, with true passion extol Him.
Let the whole creation give out another sweetness,
Nicer in our nostrils, a novel fragrance
From cleansed occasions in accord together
As one feeling fabric, all flushed and intact,
Phenomena and numbers announcing in one
Multitudinous ecumenical song
Their grand givenness of gratitude and joy,
Peaceable and plural, their positive truth
An authoritative This, an unthreatened Now
When, in love and in laughter, each lives itself,
For, united by His Word, cognition and power,
System and Order, are a single glory,
And the pattern is complex, their places safe.

W. H. Auden
Twentieth century

THE women kneeled down, lighted more candles, and from under their shawls took out wafer bread, loaves of long-bread, corn meal baked in corn husks, pans of panocha, even a cheap store sponge-cake to place on the sunken graves.

It was el Dia de los Muertos, and they had come with offerings for the dead.

They who lie here were as alive as we who have not forgotten. We too will lie here and will not be forgotten. Are we all alive, or all dead, in the unceasing file from one mystery to another, through this watery blue veil of November dusk? Let no one say. Let him say only: I am the seed of the husk that lies here, my Corn Mother; and I am the seed of those husks which will follow after me; and this meal I now place here is the bond between us all; and may our Earth Mother, our Corn Mother, attest I have not forgotten.

Frank Waters
Twentieth century

BY eating the dish of God's mercy, they anticipate the eternal meal when God, no longer in earthly symbols but in the accomplishment of his revealed glory, makes himself into the eternal meal of the redeemed.

Karl Rahner
Twentieth century

A ND then how I shall lie through centuries,
And hear the blessed mutter of the mass,
And see God made and eaten all day long,
And feel the steady candle-flame, and taste
Good strong thick stupefying incense-smoke!

Robert Browning
Nineteenth century

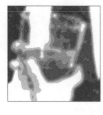

A NIMA Christi, sanctifica me.
Corpus Christi, salva me.
Sanguis Christi, inebria me.
Aqua lateris Christi, lava me.
Passio Christi, conforta me.
O bone Jesu, exaudi me.
Intra tua vulnera absconde me.
Ne permittas me separari a te.
Ab hoste maligno defende me.
In hora mortis meæ voca me.
Et jube me venire ad te.
Ut cum sanctis tuis laudem te.
In sæcula sæculorum. Amen.

S ANCTIFY me wholly, Soul of Christ adored;
Be my sure Salvation, Body of the Lord:
Fill and satisfy me, O Thou Blood unpriced:
Wash me, Sacred Water, from the side of Christ.
Passion of my Saviour, be my strength in need:
Good and gracious Jesus, to my prayer give heed:
In Thy Wounds most precious let me refuge find:
All the power malignant of the foeman bind:
At death's final hour, call me to Thy face:
Bid me stand beside Thee in the heavenly place:
There with Saints and Angels I shall sing to Thee
Through the countless ages of eternity.

Anonymous
Fourteenth century

Lord Jesus Christ,
you give us your body and blood in the eucharist
as a sign that even now we share your life.
May we come to possess it completely in the kingdom
where you live for ever and ever.   *Roman Missal*

On the day of the New Moon in the month he was to
die, the rabbi of Apt discussed at his table the death
of the righteous man. When he had said grace he rose and
began to walk back and forth in the room. His face glowed.
Then he stopped by the table and said: "Table, pure table,
you will testify in my behalf that I have properly eaten and
properly taught at your board."

Tales of the Hasidim
Later he bade that his coffin be made out of the table.   Eighteenth century

Now the green blade rises from the buried grain,
Wheat that in dark earth many days has lain;
Love lives again, that with the dead has been;   John M. C. Crum
Love is come again like wheat arising green.   Twentieth century

WHEN HE WAS AT THE TABLE WITH THEM, HE TOOK BREAD,
BLESSED AND BROKE IT, AND GAVE IT TO THEM.   Luke 24:30

~

NOW Christ our Paschal Lamb is slain,
The Lamb of God that knows no stain;
Latin hymn   The true Oblation offered here,
Seventh century   Our own unleavened Bread sincere.

LITTLE Lamb, who made thee?
Dost thou know who made thee?
Gave thee life & bid thee feed,
By the stream & o'er the mead;
Gave theee clothing of delight,
Softest clothing wooly bright;
Gave thee such a tender voice,
Making all the vales rejoice!
   Little Lamb who made thee?
   Dost thou know who made thee?

Little Lamb I'll tell thee,
Little Lamb I'll tell thee!
He is calléd by thy name,
For he calls himself a Lamb:
He is meek & he is mild,
He became a little child:
I a child & thou a lamb,
We are calléd by his name.
William Blake   Little Lamb God bless thee.
Eighteenth century   Little Lamb God bless thee.

D$_{ID}$ he who made the Lamb make thee?

William Blake
Eighteenth century

Y$_{OUR}$ lamb shall be without blemish, a year-old male; you may take it from the sheep or from the goats. You shall keep it until the fourteenth day of this month; then the whole assembled congregation of Israel shall slaughter it at twilight.

Exodus 12:5–6

S$_{ACRIFICING}$ an animal means consciously participating in cosmic movement, from life through death to life. The dead creature is eaten in the context of sharing, both with other people and with unseen supernatural forces, part of the meat being set aside to be offered up to the gods; sometimes the whole animal is destroyed and not eaten by its sacrificers, so that the gods receive all of it as a gift. ("To sacrifice" in English means "to give something up" in consequence.) Sacrificial animals are usually males, which makes sense in the context of animal husbandry, where females produce both the milk and the young. Emphasis is placed in addition on the unblemished state of the animal chosen, because generosity and not merely economics enters into the offering and eating of the sacrifice.

Margaret Visser
Twentieth century

SINCE it was the day of Preparation, the Jews did not want the bodies left on the cross during the sabbath, especially because that sabbath was a day of great solemnity. So they asked Pilate to have the legs of the crucified men broken and the bodies removed. Then the soldiers came and broke the legs of the first and of the other who had been crucified with him. But when they came to Jesus and saw that he was already dead, they did not break his legs. Instead, one of the soldiers pierced his side with a spear, and at once blood and water came out.

John 19:31–34

SING, my tongue, the Savior's glory,
Of his Flesh the mystery sing:
Of the Blood, all price exceeding,
Shed by our immortal King,
Destined, for the world's redemption,
From a noble womb to spring.

Thomas Aquinas
Thirteenth century

VERY merrily and gladly our Lord looked into his side, and he gazed and said this: See how I loved you; as if he had said: My child, if you cannot look on my divinity, see here how I suffered my side to be opened and my heart to be split in two and to send out blood and water, all that was in it; and this is a delight to me, and I wish it to be so for you.

Julian of Norwich
Fourteenth century

THE shepherd says: I pity the one
Who draws himself back from my love,
And does not seek the joy of my presence,
Though my heart is an open wound with love for him.

After a long time he climbed a tree,
And spread his shining arms,
And hung by them, and died,   John of the Cross
His heart an open wound with love.   Sixteenth century

LOOK with favor on the offering of your Church
in which we show forth the paschal sacrifice of Christ
entrusted to us.
Through the power of your Spirit of love
include us now and for ever
among the members of your Son,
whose body and blood we share.   *Roman Missal*

THAT the oblation by which the faithful offer the divine victim to the Eternal Father may have its full effect, a second
element must be added: namely, the offering of themselves   Pius XII
as victim.   Twentieth century

A ND here we offer and present to thee, O Lord, ourselves, our souls, and bodies, to be a reasonable, holy,
and lively sacrifice unto thee: humbly beseeching thee, that
whosoever shall be partakers of this holy Communion, may
worthily receive the most precious body and blood of thy
son Jesus Christ: and be fulfilled with thy grace and heavenly benediction, and made one body with thy son Jesus
Christ, that he may dwell in them and they in him.

First Prayer Book of
Edward VI
Sixteenth century

T HE oblation is ours and yet it is his.

Evelyn Underhill
Twentieth century

H AIL, altar! and thou, Victim, hail!
Thy glorious passion shall not fail;
Whereby our life no death might lack,
And life from death be rendered back.

Fortunatus
Sixth century

H E is the true and eternal priest
who established this unending sacrifice.
He offered himself as a victim for our deliverance
and taught us to make this offering in his memory.
As we eat his body which he gave for us,
we grow in strength.
As we drink his blood which he poured out for us,
we are washed clean.

Roman Missal

Y OU, O Lord, are the pleasing oblation,
who was offered for us;
you are the forgiving sacrifice,
who offered yourself for us to your Father.
You are the Lamb of sacrifice,
and yet also the priest who offered himself for us.
May our prayers be like incense in your sight
as we present them through you and with you to your Father.   Maronite liturgy

H E is the tender butcher who showed me how the price   Angela Carter
of flesh is love.   Twentieth century

T HE Word of God from heaven came,
But did not leave the Father's side;
Fulfilled his mission here on earth,
And for our sake was crucified.

The very night before he died
And to his passion he was led,
He gave to his disciples life,
His own true self in form of bread.

His body and his precious blood
He offered under either kind,
And in the fullness of his love   Thomas Aquinas
Gave food of life to humankind.   Thirteenth century

T HE dripping blood our only drink,
The bloody flesh our only food:
In spite of which we like to think   T. S. Eliot
That we are sound, substantial flesh and blood.   Twentieth century

LORD of the Powers, fill this sacrifice too
with your power and your participation.
For it is to you that we have offered
this living sacrifice, this bloodless offering.
It is to you that we have offered this bread,
figure of the body of your only-begotten Son.
This bread is a figure of the holy body.

Serapion of Thmuis
Fourth century

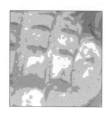

IN this sad state, Gods Tender Bowells run
Out streams of Grace; And he to end all strife
The Purest Wheate in Heaven, his deare-dear Son
Grinds, and kneads up into this Bread of Life.
Which Bread of Life from Heaven down came and stands
Disht on thy Table up by Angells Hands.

Did God mould up this Bread in Heaven, and bake,
Which from his Table came, and to thine goeth?
Doth he bespeake thee thus, This Soule Bread take.
Come Eate thy fill of this thy Gods White Loafe?
Its Food too fine for Angells, yet come, take
And Eate thy fill. Its Heavens Sugar Cake.

What Grace is this knead in this Loafe? This thing
Souls are but petty things it to admire.
Yee Angells, help: This fill would to the brim
Heav'ns whelm'd-down Chrystall meele Bowle,
yea and higher.
This Bread of Life dropt in thy mouth, doth Cry.
Eate, Eate me, Soul, and thou shalt never dy.

Edward Taylor
Seventeenth century

PENTECOST and fire are a source for the eucharist.
There is the fire of ovens,
which bakes our dough into eucharistic bread.
And there is the fire of the spirit,   Jeffrey VanderWilt
which bakes our hearts into living bread.   Twentieth century

LET me be fodder for wild beasts — that is how I can get
to God. I am God's wheat and I am being ground by the   Ignatius of Antioch
teeth of wild beasts to make a pure loaf for Christ.   First century

VERY truly, I tell you, unless a grain of wheat falls into
the earth and dies, it remains just a single grain; but if
it dies, it bears much fruit.   John 12:24

OUR life — to be eucharistic — must be wheat —
seed and soil — light and darkness,
growth and grinding —
rhythm and season — now barren, now blooming,
now barren again —   Jane Walker
eruptive force of faith and hoping.   Twentieth century

Tears are dried with bread broke open and shared.
Such power in a grain of wheat.
Living in darkness prepared for this feast.
Yet death's stone must greet the seed
and break it into fullness.
Blood wine passes lip to lip,
flooding new life with sacrifice.
The bell of remembering tolls with rhythm
and tone, heavy on the human heart.

Anita Constance
Twentieth century

Blessed are you, Lord, God of all creation. Through your goodness we have this bread to offer, which earth has given and human hands have made. It will become for us the bread of life.

Roman Missal

Consecrate this chalice mixed with wine and water.
May it become a chalice of thanksgiving and salvation
for all those who drink from it.
May it become a chalice
which is a pledge of new life for us.
May it become a chalice which unites us
to the guests of your banquet.
May it become a chalice which opens to us
the gates of your heavenly kingdom.
May it forgive our faults and pardon our sins.
Through it may we become sharers
with the faithful departed
in the joy which will never end.

Maronite liturgy

Fᴉʟʟ high the bowl, and spice it well, and pour
The dews oblivious: for the Cross is sharp,
    The Cross is sharp, and He
    Is tenderer than a lamb.

John Keble
Nineteenth century

Aɴ ancient Greek libation was a sort of concrete prayer,
a sharing of wine with the gods. The Homeric ritual for
this act entailed rising to one's feet holding a cup full of
wine in the right hand, looking up into the sky, deliberately
spilling some of the liquid, praying with both arms and cup
raised, then drinking. The Olympian gods were not neces-
sarily thought to have imbibed the wine—but they accepted
the gift, the sacrifice of that all-important first mouthful,
and a connection with them was thereby established.

Margaret Visser
Twentieth century

Iɴ the dark, the girl came by and I asked her to take drinks
to the bandstand. There was a long pause, while they
talked up there in the indigo light and after awhile I saw the
girl put a Scotch and milk on top of the piano for Sonny.
He didn't seem to notice it, but just before they started play-
ing again, he sipped from it and look toward me, and nodded. Then he put it back on top of the piano. For me, then,
as they began to play again, it glowed and shook above my
brother's head like the very cup of trembling.

James Baldwin
Twentieth century

COME slowly — Eden!
Lips unused to Thee —
Bashful — sip thy Jessamines —
As the fainting Bee —

Reaching late his flower,
Round her chamber hums —
Counts his nectars —
Enters — and is lost in Balms.

Emily Dickinson
Nineteenth century

THEN the mother of the sons of Zebedee came to him with her sons, and kneeling before him, she asked a favor of him. And he said to her, "What do you want?" She said to him, "Declare that these two sons of mine will sit, one at your right hand and one at your left, in your kingdom." But Jesus answered, "You do not know what you are asking. Are you able to drink the cup that I am about to drink?" They said to him, "We are able." He said to them, "You will indeed drink my cup, but to sit at my right hand and at my left, this is not mine to grant, but it is for those for whom it has been prepared by my Father."

Matthew 20:20 – 23

To drink the blood of Jesus is to partake of the Lord's immortality; and the Spirit is the strength of the Word, as blood is the strength of flesh.

Clement of Alexandria
Second century

B Y this they made it clear that it was by the blood of the
Lord that redemption was going to come to all who   Clement of Rome
believe in God and hope on him.   First century

W OULD you be free from your burden of sin?
There's power in the blood,
power in the blood;
Would you o'er evil a victory win?
There's wonderful power in the blood.
There is power, power,
Wonder-working power
In the blood of the Lamb;
There is power, power,
Wonder-working power   Lewis E. Jones
In the precious blood of the Lamb.   Nineteenth century

Y OUR blood, a God's blood, you poured over the earth,
sealing a blood-bargain   Hippolytus of Rome
for humanity because you loved them.   Second century

B LOOD of Jesus Christ,
who became flesh for us,
   who was born of the holy Virgin.

Blood of Jesus Christ,
   who was born of the holy Mother of God.

Blood of Jesus Christ,
   who manifested himself in the flesh.

Blood of Jesus Christ,
   who was baptized in the Jordan
   by the Precursor.
   Jesus Christ! Amen.

Blood of Jesus Christ,
   who offered himself as a victim
Anonymous   for our sins.
Fifth century   Jesus Christ! Amen.

Y OU are there on the table; you are there in the chalice.
You are this body with us, for, collectively, we are this
Augustine of Hippo   body. We drink of the same chalice because we live the
Fourth century   same life.

B ᴜᴛ this thing then that has plenty

Understands together fails not
Of future nor frees its past thought
And so mighty that all be right
To touch in the middle of light

Pleasance and presence of trace
A feathering moving a face
Who are mine having nothing to save
For your grace such it cannot but have.

Louis Zukofsky
Twentieth century

W ʜᴇɴ the roast was well under way, Black Tom, very formal in a white waistcoat and high collar, poured the champagne. Captain Forrester lifted his glass, the frail stem between his thick fingers, and glancing round the table at his guests and at Mrs. Forrester, said,

"Happy days!"

It was the toast he always drank at dinner, the invocation he was sure to utter when he took a glass of whiskey with an old friend. Whoever had heard him say it once, liked to hear him say it again. Nobody else could utter those two words as he did, with such gravity and high courtesy.

Willa Cather
Twentieth century

T ʜᴇɴ they restored their strength with food and reclining on the grass they piled the tables high with vituals and passed the cup. Afterwards rest came, the tables were removed, and he himself was among the first to honor the Father, looking toward heaven. Tongues grew silent. He gives with his hands fruit, and sweet water from a font, and he filled a bowl with wine, and he taught them the rite of the celebration.

Proba
Fourth century

B EN knew there was work to be done because they had not changed and the sadness was still there. He raised his hands for the great silence. And they gave it.

"It will be the last time I will ever sing for them," he thought. "I must make it good." And it was.

He sang colors they had never seen, in a land they had never seen. He even sang a giraffe, and that, not even he had ever seen. He sang sugar cane from another country, melons and cherries and all summer fruit in the winter snow, still fresh and good. He sang a man singing another man singing another man, and babies born in times to come. And oxen and warm fire and the sea gulls along the shore. And on and on he sang the Promised Land. The weary, he sang rested. The hungry, he sang full. The cold, he sang warm. And the great sadness, he sang all away. And then he sang no more.

Then the people knelt down and he saw the King standing among them. Now the King knew that Ben was innocent and set him free. He put his hand on the boy's shoulder and promised all the people in the meadow that he would make that song come true. That he would travel among them and feel their pain and change their lives to fit the beautiful song. Never again would he go to war in foreign lands but rather, he would stay among his own people and help them. This was the first decision he had ever made alone. At last, he had found a truly just cause.

Seymour Leichman
Twentieth century

Then, they all sat down together and had a simply marvelous breakfast in the meadow.

Goᴅ has enough of all good things
    except one:
Of communion with humans
    God can never have enough.

Mechthild of Magdeburg
Thirteenth century

Wʜɪʟᴇ they were eating, Jesus took a loaf of bread, and after blessing it he broke it, gave it to the disciples, and said, "Take, eat; this is my body." Then he took a cup, and after giving thanks he gave it to them, saying, "Drink from it, all of you; for this is my blood of the covenant, which is poured out for many for the forgiveness of sins. I tell you, I will never again drink of this fruit of the vine until that day when I drink it new with you in my Father's kingdom." Matthew 26:26–29

HE SAID TO THEM, "HAVE YOU ANYTHING HERE TO EAT?" THEY
GAVE HIM A PIECE OF BROILED FISH, AND HE TOOK IT AND ATE IN
THEIR PRESENCE.   Luke 24:41b–43

~

ON the night of that Last Supper
Seated with his chosen band,
He, the Paschal victim eating,
First fulfills the Law's command;

Thomas Aquinas   Then as food to his apostles
Thirteenth century Gives himself with his own hand.

Joseph Campbell
Twentieth century   WE wouldn't be here if we weren't eating.

Lord Byron
Nineteenth century SINCE Eve ate apples, much depends on dinner.

THEN the big part happens. Instead of everyone running up'n grabbin' plates'n divin' into it, somethin' real big happens. Big but simple, eh? Young men, warriors, braves, whatever you wanna call 'em, get up outta the circl'n start servin' the people. Drummers'n singers are singing an honor song for the people an' the young men start servin' 'em. Start with the elders. Old guys like me and the old women get to eat first. It helps us remember that we gotta respect the wisdom of them that lived long time. Respect their vision. What they seen'n learned from. The teachin's they hold. Reason the young men serve the people's to remind them of their place. Be humble. Warrior's gotta be people's protectors. Biggest part of protectin' is nurturin'. Helpin' the people. Bein' humble enough to feed 'em first. It's another sly part. Reminds 'em that warriors gotta learn to nurture before they learn to fight or hunt or anythin'. Biggest part of protectin' is nurturin'. Feedin' the people first. Takin' care of 'em. Mother's side workin' in them young men. That's why they do that.

After the elders are served the young men feed the women'n children. Once everyone's served they sit an' feed themselves. Women get up after'n fill bowls up. Go around'n round again and again until all the food's gone. Sly again. Reminds us there ain't no such things as better or bigger. Equal. Share the responsibility. Men'n women gotta be equals. That's what that simple sharin' of responsibility reminds us of. Equals. Two sides balanced in that circle. Makin' it complete. Two sides balanced inside us too.

Richard Wagamese
Twentieth century

ON this mountain the LORD of
hosts will make for all peoples
a feast of rich food, a feast of
well-aged wines,
of rich food filled with marrow,
of well-aged wines strained clear.

Isaiah 25:6

GILGAMESH, fill your belly with good things; day and night, night and day, dance and be merry, feast and rejoice. Let your clothes be fresh, bathe yourself in water, cherish the little child that holds your hand, and make your wife happy in your embrace; for this too is the lot of man.

The Epic of Gilgamesh
Second millennium BCE

THE Lord gave himself to us precisely as food to be enjoyed.

Karl Rahner
Twentieth century

ART is a matter of enjoyment through the five senses. Unless you can see the beauty all around you everywhere, and enjoy it, you can never comprehend art. . . . Esthetic appreciation begins with the enjoyment of the morning bath.

Willa Cather
Twentieth century

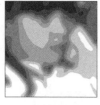

AND Eve, within, due at her hour, prepared
For dinner savoury fruits, of taste to please
True appetite, and not disrelish thirst
Of nectarous draughts between, from milky stream,
Berry or grape.

John Milton
Seventeenth century

THE work done, the feast laid out, they ate well
and no man's hunger lacked a share of the banquet.

Homer
Ninth century BCE

THEN the LORD said to Moses, "I am going to rain bread from heaven for you, and each day the people shall go out and gather enough for that day."

Exodus 16:4

GOD gave them plenty
they ate a giant's portion.

Psalm 78:25

REV. J. B. Schlund's Angel Food Cake:
  2 lbs. sugar
  8 oz. corn starch
  42 oz. flour
  ½ oz. cream of tartar
  1 quart of egg whites

The recipe book of
David A. Woods
Twentieth century

ALLELUIA! Bread of Angels,
Here on earth our food, our stay!
Alleluia! here the sinful
Flee to you from day to day:
Intercessor, friend of sinners,
Earth's redeemer, plead for me,
Where the songs of all the sinless
Sweep across the crystal sea.

William C. Dix
Nineteenth century

THEY said to him, "Sir, give us this bread always."

Jesus said to them, "I am the bread of life. Whoever comes to me will never be hungry, and whoever believes in me will never be thirsty."

John 6:34–35

YOU satisfy the hungry heart
With gift of finest wheat;
Come give to us, O saving Lord,
The bread of life to eat.

Omer Westendorf
Twentieth century

O God, you fed not only us from our youth but also
every living creature. Feed our hungry souls, we pray,
with heavenly food: for you are the one who fills the hungry with good things.

Ulrich Zwingli
Sixteenth century

WE taste thee, O thou living Bread,
And long to feast upon thee still;
We drink of thee, the fountain-head,
And thirst our souls from thee to fill.

Attributed to Bernard
of Clairvaux
Twelfth century

EAT this bread, drink this cup,
come to me and never be hungry.
Eat this bread, drink this cup,
trust in me and you will not thirst.

Jacques Berthier
Twentieth century

WHO would suppose, from Adam's simple ration,
That cookery could have call'd forth such resources.

Lord Byron
Nineteenth century

Y OU probably need to eat something," the baker said. "I
    hope you'll eat some of my hot rolls. You have to eat
and keep going. Eating is a small, good thing in a time like
this," he said.

He served them warm cinnamon rolls just out of the oven,
the icing still runny. He put butter on the table and knives
to spread the butter. Then the baker sat down at the table
with them. He waited. He waited until they each took a roll
from the platter and began to eat. "It's good to eat something," he said, watching them. "There's more. Eat up. Eat all
you want. There's all the rolls in the world in here."

They ate rolls and drank coffee. Ann was suddenly hungry,
and the rolls were warm and sweet. She ate three of them,
which pleased the baker. Then he began to talk. They listened carefully. Although they were tired and in anguish,
they listened to what the baker had to say. They nodded
when the baker began to speak of loneliness, and of the
sense of doubt and limitation that had come to him in his
middle years. He told them what it was like to be childless
all these years. To repeat the days with the ovens endlessly
full and endlessly empty. The party food, the celebrations
he'd worked over. Icing knuckle-deep. The tiny wedding
couples stuck into cakes. Hundreds of them, no, thousands
by now. Birthdays. Just imagine all those candles burning.
He had a necessary trade. He was a baker. He was glad he
wasn't a florist. It was better to be feeding people. This was
a better smell anytime than flowers.

"Smell this," the baker said, breaking open a dark loaf. "It's
a heavy bread, but rich." They smelled it, then he had them
taste it. It had the taste of molasses and coarse grains. They
listened to him. They ate what they could. They swallowed
the dark bread. It was like daylight under the fluorescent
trays of light. They talked on into the early morning, the
high, pale cast of light in the windows, and they did not
think of leaving.

Raymond Carver
Twentieth century

Paul Bernier
Twentieth century

IF we understand eucharist as the mystery of Christ's continuing ability to feed his people, if we know that his bread is broken to be shared with the needy and the poor, this will form our attitude and lend the dynamism of faith to our efforts. We need a clear ideal of what kind of world we are striving to build, and the ideal we take from the Lord's table is that he has given us brothers and sisters the world over who have a claim on us because we accept the bread broken in order to be shared.

Robert Griffin
Twentieth century

HE chooses to identify himself with the hungry, the thirsty, the naked, and the prisoner, so that we may serve him and touch him in times of famine and drought, and in the ghettos and jails. God is constantly invading our world with his nearness. Is it any wonder then that he takes bread and wine, the staples of the table with which he feeds us, and surrounds and endows them with his life?

Isaiah 51:14

THE oppressed shall speedily be released;
they shall not die and go down to the Pit,
nor shall they lack bread.

Augustine of Hippo
Fourth century

THERE feeding the angels, here on earth a hungry Child; there unfailing Bread with perfect powers, here, along with speechless children, needing the nourishment of milk; there doing good, here suffering evil; there never dying, here rising after death and bestowing eternal life on mortals. God became one of us so that we might become God.

As honey drips from the honeycomb of bees,
And milk flows from the woman
    who loves her children,
So also is my hope upon thee, O my God.

The Odes of Solomon
Second century

THIS Earth is the honey of all Beings, and all Beings
Are the honey of this Earth . . . O bright immortal Lover
That is incarnate in the body's earth —
O bright immortal Lover who is All!

Edith Sitwell
Twentieth century

THE Pedigree of Honey
Does not concern the Bee —
A Clover, any time, to him,
Is Aristocracy —

Emily Dickinson
Nineteenth century

SURROUNDED by clay pitchers, Manuela Sáenz reigns in
the shaded portico of her house. Beyond, among moun-
tains the color of death, extends the Bay of Paita. Exiled in
this Peruvian port, Manuela lives by making sweets and fruit
preserves. Ships stop to buy. Her goodies enjoy great fame
on these coasts. Whalers sigh for a spoonful.

Eduardo Galeano
Twentieth century

Heaped up on the floor, to form a kind of throne, were turkeys, geese, game, poultry, brawn, great joints of meat, sucking-pigs, long wreaths of sausages, mince-pies, plum-puddings, barrels of oysters, red-hot chestnuts, cherry-cheeked apples, juicy oranges, luscious pears, immense twelfth-cakes, and seething bowls of punch, that made the chambers dim with their delicious steam. In easy state upon this couch, there sat a jolly Giant, glorious to see who bore a glowing torch, in shape not unlike Plenty's horn, and held it up, high up, to shed its light on Scrooge, as he came peeping round the door.

"Come in!" exclaimed the Ghost — "come in! and know me better, man!"

Charles Dickens
Nineteenth century

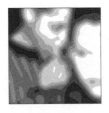

Let my Beloved come, and taste
His pleasant Fruits at his own Feast.
I come, my Spouse, I come, he cries,
With Love and Pleasure in his Eyes.

Our Lord into his Garden comes,
Well pleas'd to smell our poor Perfumes,
And calls us to a Feast divine,
Sweeter than Honey, Milk, or Wine.

Eat of the Tree of Life, my Friends,
The Blessings that my Father sends;
Your Taste shall all my Dainties prove,
And drink abundance of my Love.

Jesus, we will frequent thy Board,
And sing the Bounties of our Lord:
But the rich Food on which we live
Demands more Praise than Tongues can give.

Isaac Watts
Eighteenth century

H E makes the Figs our mouths to meet,
And throws the Melons at our feet;
But Apples plants of such a price,
No tree could ever bear them twice.

Andrew Marvell
Seventeenth century

A s the vintages of earth
Taste of the sun that riped their birth,
We know what never-cadent Sun
Thy lampèd clusters throbbed upon,
What plumed feet the winepress trod;
Thy wine is flavorous of God.

Francis Thompson
Nineteenth century

I taste a liquor never brewed —
From Tankards scooped in Pearl —
Not all the Vats upon the Rhine
Yield such an Alcohol!

Inebriate of Air — am I —
And Debauchee of Dew —
Reeling — thro endless summer days —
From inns of Molten Blue —

When "Landlords" turn the drunken Bee
Out of the Foxglove's door —
When Butterflies — renounce their "drams" —
I shall but drink the more!

Till Seraphs swing their snowy Hats —
And Saints — to windows run —
To see the little Tippler
Leaning against the — Sun —

Emily Dickinson
Nineteenth century

WINE possesses a sparkle, a perfume, a vigor, that expands and clears the imagination. Under the form of wine Christ gives us his divine blood. It is no plain and sober draught. It was bought at a great price, at a divinely excessive price.

Romano Guardini
Twentieth century

IN the inner wine cellar
I drank of my Beloved, and, when I went abroad
Through all this valley
I no longer knew anything,
And lost the herd which I was following.

There he gave me his breast;
There he taught me a sweet and living knowledge;
And I gave myself to him,
Keeping nothing back;
There I promised to be His bride.

John of the Cross
Sixteenth century

ALL the same when Martine saw a barrow load of bottles wheeled into the kitchen, she stood still. She touched the bottles and lifted up one. "What is there in this bottle, Babette?" she asked in a low voice. "Not wine?" "Wine, Madame!" Babette answered. "No, Madame. It is a Clos Vougeot 1846!" After a moment she added: "From Philippe, in Rue Montorgueil!" Martine had never suspected that wines could have names to them, and was put to silence.

Isak Dinesen
Twentieth century

G IVE strong drink to one who is perishing,
and wine to those in bitter distress;
let them drink and forget their poverty,
and remember their misery no more.

Proverbs 31:6–7

C OME, O faithful: let us drink a new drink, produced
miraculously not from a barren rock, but springing from
the tomb which is a fountain of immortality: the tomb of
Christ by which we are strengthened.

Orthodox liturgy

C OME, let us taste the Vine's new fruit,
For heavenly joy preparing;
To-day the branches with the Root
   In Resurrection sharing:
Whom as true God our hymns adore
For ever and for evermore.

John Damascene
Eighth century

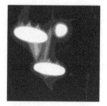

W HILE yet a child, Abba Ephrem had a dream and then
a vision. A branch of vine came out of his tongue,
grew bigger and filled everything under heaven. It was laden
with beautiful fruit. All the birds of heaven came to eat of
the fruit of the vine, and the more they ate, the more the
fruit increased.

*Sayings of the
Desert Fathers*

So the priest trusted in the promise of St. Francis and freely let the people who came there take and eat the grapes. It certainly is a wonderful thing that the vineyard was completely stripped and ruined by them, so that only a few little bunches of grapes remained. But when the vintage came, the priest, trusting in the Saint's promise, gathered those little bunches of grapes and put them in the wine press and pressed them. And as St. Francis had promised, he obtained twenty measures of the very best wine that year.

The Little Flowers of St. Francis
Fourteenth century

OUR life—to be eucharistic— must be grape—
vine and branch—alone and together—
grafted and growing—
grape-pressed and given to one another.

Our life—to be eucharistic—must be wine—
free and flowing—tasted and tested—
whole and healing—cup and spilling—
wine, strengthening and sustaining, joyous communion.

Jane Walker
Twentieth century

I would like to have the inhabitants of Heaven
In my own house:
With vats of good cheer
Laid out for them.

I would like to have the three Marys,
Their fame is so great.
I would like people
From every corner of Heaven.

I would like them to be cheerful
In their drinking,
I would like to have Jesus too
Here amongst them.

I would like a great lake of beer
For the King of Kings,
I would like to be watching Heaven's family
Drinking it through all eternity.

Celtic poem
Tenth or eleventh
century

GREET chiere made oure Hoost us everichon,
And to the soper sette he us anon.
He served us with vitaille at the beste;
Strong was the wyn, and wel to drynke us leste.

Geoffrey Chaucer
Fourteenth century

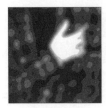

WHILE spoon-feeding him with one hand
she holds his hand with her other hand,
or rather lets it rest on top of his,
which is permanently clenched shut.
When he turns his head away, she reaches
around and puts in the spoonful blind.
He will not accept the next morsel
until he has completely chewed this one.
His bright squint tells her he finds
the shrimp she has just put in delicious.
Next to the voice and touch of those we love,
food may be our last pleasure on earth —
a man on death row takes his T-bone
in small bites and swishes each sip
of the jug wine around in his mouth,
tomorrow will be too late for them to jolt
this supper out of him.

Galway Kinnell
Twentieth century

ON the table, then — *any* table — there is never just food.
There is, rather, the whole history of creation struggling
toward consciousness, of peripheries pushing toward a center, of stone seeking speech, of wood waiting for something
or someone to carry. On the table — *any* table — lies a stag-
gering history of needs felt, met or denied; of stammered
confessions; of hands groping for the last crust of bread;
of goblets glowing, lifted and struck; of accusations and
reprieves; of lost children and drowned lovers.

Nathan D. Mitchell
Twentieth century

During the retreat even meals were held in silence, with the ancient monastic practice of table reading. As we ate, a sister read to us from an excellent essay on ecology. Meals in common were holy to Saint Benedict, and Benedictine life aims for continuity between church and dining hall, a continuity that silence tends to amplify. As we scraped and stacked our dishes I noted that, as is usual with monastic people, very little food was wasted. You take what you need and eat what you take. The article reminded us that we all have a long way to go, but we could see that there was a connection between what we had been praying in church and practicing at our meal.

Kathleen Norris
Twentieth century

GIVE us this day our daily bread.

Matthew 6:11

VERY bread, good shepherd, tend us,
Jesu, of your love befriend us,
You refresh us, you defend us,
Your eternal goodness send us
In the land of life to see.

You who all things can and know,
Who on earth such food bestow,
Grant us with your saints, though lowest,
Where the heav'nly feast you show,
Fellow heirs and guests to be. Amen. Alleluia.

Sequence of
Corpus Christi

THEN THEIR EYES WERE OPENED, AND THEY RECOGNIZED HIM.

Luke 24:31a

~

Psalm 34:9

Drink in the richness of God,
enjoy the strength of the Lord.

FOR, ere he died, the Crucified
    Wrought things eternal for us
By bread and wine, which Love divine
    Hath given to assure us:
O taste and see; find him to be
Our great reward, our living Lord
    Most willing to restore us.

Adam Fox
Twentieth century

YOUR death is the sacrifice which reconciles heaven and
earth, the sacrifice in which we are all sacrificed, given
up to God, torn from ourselves, made a part of the transi-
tion and taken up also into the invisible burning flame of the
spirit, which protects and sanctifies the world and brings it
in salvation to God, even while it burns.

Karl Rahner
Twentieth century

I am a sacrifice bound with cords to the horns of the world's rock altar, waiting for worms. I take a deep breath, I open my eyes. Looking, I see there are worms in the horns of the altar like live maggots in amber, there are shells of worms in the rock and moths flapping at my eyes. A wind from noplace rises. A sense of the real exults me; the cords loose; I walk on my way.

Annie Dillard
Twentieth century

HAIL, saving Victim, offered for me and all human-kind upon the gibbet of the Cross. Hail, noble and precious blood, flowing from the wounds of my crucified Lord Jesus Christ, and washing away the sins of the whole world. Remember, O Lord, Your creatures whom You have redeemed with Your Blood.

Ambrose of Milan
Fourth century

GOD has created bountiful waters on the earth for our use and our bodily comfort, out of the tender love he has for us. But it is more pleasing to him that we accept freely his blessed blood to wash us of our sins, for there is no drink that is made which it pleases him so well to give us; for it is so plentiful, and it is of our own nature.

Julian of Norwich
Fourteenth century

FOR Jesus shed his precious blood
Rich blessings to bestow;
Come now unto that fount which flowed
That washes white as snow.

Come to Jesus,
Come to Jesus,
Come to Jesus now;
He will save you,
He will save you,
He will save you now.

John Hart Stockton
Nineteenth century

THE dying thief rejoiced to see
That fountain in his day;
And there have I, as vile as he,
    Washed all my sins away.

Dear dying Lamb, thy precious Blood
    Shall never lose its power,
Till all the ransomed Church of God
    Be saved to sin no more.

William Cowper
Eighteenth century

OH, purer than the morning ray,
Celestial Lamb, thou comest to bear
Our sins, and wash our guilt away,
    That we with thee, God's love may share.

O Fount of Love! O power divine!
    We bow before thy holy might;
Thy word makes water pour as wine;
    Thy love brings day unto our night.

Sedulius
Sixth century

CANCEL out our sins today, then,
O true God,
and wash our souls' face
with your only-begotten Son's blood,
poured out for us,
so that dead to ourselves
and living for him
we may offer him a return for his suffering
with bright face
and undivided soul.

Catherine of Siena
Fourteenth century

HE breaks the power of canceled sin,
He sets the prisoner free;
His blood can make the foulest clean —
    His blood availed for me.

See all your sins on Jesus laid:
    The Lamb of God was slain,
His soul was once an offering made
    For every soul of man.

Charles Wesley
Eighteenth century

YOU bought us back
with the pure and precious blood
of your only Son,
freed us from lies and error,
from bitter enslavement,
released us from the Devil's clutches
and gave us the glory of freedom.

Anonymous
Fourth or fifth century

I'D prefer, right now, to see one of those bright Byzantine
Christs come striding across from the opposite hills

and in this regard time shall be made of the essence

fresh from baptizing Adam, vast and masterful,
lugging a patriarch along with each arm no doubt
from some new-harrowed hell
and scattering from his feet a fine debris
of locks, bolts, spancels, cuffs, gyves, fetters, stocks,
and other miscellaneous hindrances

and in this regard time shall be made of the essence

Trevor Joyce
Twentieth century

And what would our Neighborhood Watch do then?

EVIL has power, even if that power is usually illusory or
fleeting. God, too, has power, greater power than the
Devil, and the eucharist—along with ascesis, prayer, hospitality, and works of love—is a channel, perhaps the greatest
channel, of God's power.

Tim Vivian
Twentieth century

ANYONE who enters at all earnestly and sympathetically
into the liturgical life of the church will discover there
unsuspected riches, while he may also have some of his
own narrowness and prejudice removed.

Norman Pittenger
Twentieth century

THE two old women who had once slandered each other now in their hearts went back a long way, past the evil period in which they had been stuck, to those days of their early girlhood when together they had been preparing for confirmation and hand in hand had filled the roads round Berlevaag with singing. A Brother in the congregation gave another a knock in the ribs, like a rough caress between boys, and cried out: "You cheated me on that timber, you old scoundrel!" The Brother thus addressed almost collapsed in a heavenly burst of laughter, but tears ran from his eyes. "Yes, I did so, beloved Brother," he answered. "I did so." Skipper Halvorsen and Madam Oppegaarden suddenly found themselves close together in a corner and gave one another that long, long kiss, for which the secret uncertain love affair of their youth had never left them time.

Isak Dinesen
Twentieth century

TWO youths who were deeply devoted to each other used to go to Rabbi Naftali together to sit at his table. When he distributed the bread, for such was his custom, he always gave the two friends twin loaves clinging each to each. Once they were vexed with each other. They did not know how this feeling had entered their hearts and could not overcome it. Soon after when they again went to Roptchitz and were seated at the rabbi's table on the eve of the sabbath, he took the twin loaves, cut them apart, and gave one to each of the youths. On their way home from the meal they were overcome with emotion and both cried out in the same breath: "We are at fault, we are at fault!" They went to an inn, ordered schnapps and drank a toast to each other. The next day at the midday meal of the sabbath Rabbi Naftali again put twin loaves into the hands of the friends.

Tales of the Hasidim
Eighteenth century

THE rood of dreams became a table of dreams. For both cross and meal had the same purpose: healing, reconciliation, bonding among all those whose elbows rest on the same wood, whose hands break the same bread, whose lips draw comfort from the same cup.

Nathan D. Mitchell
Twentieth century

So you plan to take a little church in Alabama, Father, preach the gospel, turn bread into flesh, forgive the sins of Buick dealers, administer communion to suburban housewives?

Walker Percy
Twentieth century

I am not worthy, Master and Lord, that you should come beneath the roof of my soul: yet, since in your love toward all, you wish to dwell in me, in boldness I come. You command, Open the gates — which you alone have forged; and you will come in with love toward all, as is your nature; you will come in and enlighten my darkened reasoning. I believe that you will do this: for you did not send away the harlot who came to you with tears; nor cast out the repenting publican; nor reject the thief who acknowledged kingdom; nor forsake the repentant persecutor, a yet greater act; but all of those who came to you in repentance, you counted in the band of your friends, who alone abides blessed forever, now, and unto the endless ages.

John Chrysostom
Fourth century

YOU shall worship the LORD your God, and I will bless your bread and your water; and I will take sickness away from among you.

Exodus 23:25

BREAK one loaf, which is the medicine of immortality, and the antidote which wards off death but yields continuous life in union with Jesus Christ.

Ignatius of Antioch
First century

LET us therefore understand that this sacrament is a medicine for the spiritually poor and sick, and that the only worthiness which our Saviour requires in us is to know ourselves, so as to be dissatisfied with our vices, and have all our pleasure, joy and contentment in him alone.

John Calvin
Sixteenth century

A woman whose little daughter had an unclean spirit immediately heard about him, and she came and bowed down at his feet. Now the woman was a Gentile, of Syrophoenician origin. She begged him to cast the demon out of her daughter. He said to her, "Let the children be fed first, for it is not fair to take the children's food and throw it to the dogs." But she answered him, "Sir, even the dogs under the table eat the children's crumbs." Then he said to her, "For saying that, you may go—the demon has left your daughter." So she went home, found the child lying on the bed, and the demon gone.

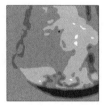

Mark 7:25–30

H ERE let each afflicted soul
Come in hope, though filled with grief;
To the sick, not to the whole,
The Physician brings relief;
Fear not therefore, but draw nigh,
Christ will all your wants supply.

John Huss
Fourteenth century

Ambrose of Milan
Fourth century

T HAT daily bread is taken as a remedy for daily infirmity.

B LOOD that bled into a cry!
The elements
felt its touch and trembled,
heaven heard their woe.
O life-blood of the maker,
scarlet music, salve our wounds.

Hildegard of Bingen
Twelfth century

H E drank some more wine and raised his face to the daz-
zle of the sun among the leaves and felt his youth lift
him and make him buoyant. He was young and healthy and
he loved and was loved. It was impossible for him, as he sat
there in the green southern light and waited for Axel, not to
feel in his veins the warm anticipation of a new happiness.

Iris Murdoch
Twentieth century

Lucy Texada Roberts' Custard:
1 quart sweet milk
3 eggs
1 cup sugar
1 Tbl. vanilla
dash of salt

Heat milk, sugar, and salt until skim forms. Slowly add beaten eggs. Cook 10 – 12 minutes or until it coats a silver spoon. Cool and add vanilla.

Aunt Martha would prepare this and bring it over to anyone who was ailing, no matter what the ailment.

Anne B. Parks
Twentieth century

O God of Truth, let your holy Word come upon this bread, that the bread may become Body of the Word, and upon this cup, that the cup may become Blood of the Truth; and make all who communicate to receive a medicine of life for the healing of every sickness and for the strengthening of all advancement and virtue, not for condemnation, O God of Truth, and not for censure and reproach. For we have invoked you, the uncreated, through the Only-begotten in the Holy Spirit.

Serapion of Thmuis
Fourth century

To heal the sick one's malady:
No wonder this our meal we make,
Since, eating it, no law we break.
'Tis as delicious as 'tis good —
A very miracle of food.

A Baghdad
Cookery Book

F ROM at least the fourteenth century, Europeans had dined on an aromatic, sweet, golden food, which revealed the strong influence of the Arabic world. These fragrant, jewel-like dishes were thought to be connected to celestial substance through their luster, odor, and color, and so to have divine healing powers.

T. Sara Peterson
Twentieth century

T HEN St. Francis immediately had water boiled with many sweet-scented herbs. Next, he undressed the man with leprosy and began to wash him with his holy hands, while another friar poured the water over him.

And by a divine miracle, wherever St. Francis touched him with his holy hands, the leprosy disappeared, and the flesh remained completely healed.

And as externally the water washed his body and the flesh began to heal and be wholly cleansed from leprosy, so too interiorly his soul began to be healed and cleansed. And when the man with leprosy saw himself being healed externally, he immediately began to have great compunction and remorse for his sins. And he began to cry very bitterly. Just as his body was washed with water and cleansed from leprosy, so his conscience was baptized by tears and contrition and cleansed from all evil and sin.

The Little Flowers
of St. Francis
Fourteenth century

When he was completely washed and healed physically, he was perfectly anointed and healed spiritually.

I T was said of Abba John the Persian that when some evil-doers came to him, he took a basin and wanted to wash their feet. But they were filled with confusion, and began to do penance.

Sayings of the
Desert Fathers

M AY I become a medicine for the sick and their physician, their support until sickness come not again.

May I become an unfailing store for the wretched, and be first to supply them with their needs.

My own self and my pleasures, my righteousness past, present and future, may I sacrifice without regard, in order to achieve the welfare of beings.

Santideva
Seventh century

I N these acts of giving do not fear a lack of means. A generous spirit is itself great wealth. There can be no shortage of material for generosity where it is Christ who feeds and Christ who is fed. In all this activity there is present the hand of him who multiplies the bread by breaking it, and increases it by giving it away.

Leo the Great
Fifth century

N O picnic party; the whites found themselves at once surrounded by, gazed at, gazing into the faces of these blacks who had stoned white drivers on the main road, who had taken control of this place out of the hands of white authority, who refused to pay for the right to exist in the decaying ruins of the war of attrition against their presence too close across the veld; these people who killed police collaborators, in their impotence to stop the police killing their children. One thing to read about them in the papers, to empathize with them, across the veld; Hannah felt the fear in her companions like a rise in temperature inside the vehicle. She slid open the window beside her. Instead of stones, black hands reached in, met and touched first hers and then those of all inside who reached out to them. The windows were opened. Passengers jostled one another for the blessing of the hands, the healing touch.

Nadine Gordimer
Twentieth century

ONE of the crowd went up,
And knelt before the Paten and the Cup,
Received the Lord, returned in peace, and prayed
Close to my side. Then in my heart I said:

"O Christ, in this man's life—
This stranger who is Thine—in all his strife,
All his felicity, his good and ill,
In the assaulted stronghold of his will,

"I do confess Thee here,
Alive within this life; I know Thee near
Within this lonely conscience, closed away
Within this brother's solitary day.

"Christ in his unknown heart,
His intellect unknown—this love, this art,
This battle and this peace, this destiny
That I shall never know, look upon me!

"Christ in his numbered breath,
Christ in his beating heart and in his death,
Christ in his mystery! From that secret place
And from that separate dwelling, give me grace!"

Alice Meynell
Nineteenth century

THE abundance of this place,
the songs of its people and its birds,
will be health and wisdom and indwelling
light. This is no paradisal dream.
Its hardship is its possibility.

Wendell Berry
Twentieth century

COME, my Light, and illumine my darkness.
Come, my Life, and revive me from death.
Come, my Physician, and heal my wounds.
Come, Flame of divine love, and burn up the thorns
    of my sins,
  kindling my heart with the flame of thy love.
Come, my King, sit upon the throne of my heart
    and reign there.
For thou alone art my King and my Lord.

Dimitrii of Rostov
Seventeenth century

ALMIGHTY, everlasting God, I draw near to the sacrament of your only-begotten Son, our Lord Jesus Christ. I who am sick approach to the physician of life. I who am unclean come to the fountain of mercy; blind to the light of eternal brightness; poor and needy, to the Lord of heaven and earth. Therefore, I implore you, in your boundless mercy, to heal my sickness, cleanse my defilement, enlighten my blindness, enrich my poverty, and clothe my nakedness. Then shall I dare to receive the bread of angels, the King of kings and Lord of lords, with reverence and humility, contrition and love, purity and faith, with the purpose and intention necessary for the good of my soul.

Thomas Aquinas
Thirteenth century

STRENGTHEN, O Lord, the hands that holy things have taken, that they may daily bring forth fruit to thy glory. Grant, O Lord, that the lips which have sung thy praise within the sanctuary, may glorify thee for ever; that the ears which have heard the voice of thy songs, may be closed to the voice of clamour and dispute; that the eyes which have seen thy great love, may also behold thy blessed hope; that the tongues which have sung the sanctus, may ever speak the truth. Grant that the feet that have trod in thy holy courts may ever walk in the light, and that the souls and bodies, which have tasted of thy living body and blood, may ever be restored in newness of life.

Liturgy of Malabar

THAT SAME HOUR THEY GOT UP AND RETURNED TO JERUSALEM;
AND THEY FOUND THE ELEVEN AND THEIR COMPANIONS GATH-
ERED TOGETHER. THEN THEY TOLD WHAT HAD HAPPENED ON
THE ROAD.   Luke 24:33, 35

~

IT prospered strangely, and did soon disperse
          Through all the earth;
    For they that taste it do rehearse
       That virtue, lies therein;
A secret virtue, bringing peace and mirth
          By flight of sin.

Take of this grain, which in my garden grows,
          And grows for you;
    Make bread of it; and that repose
       And peace, which everywhere
With so much earnestness you do pursue,   George Herbert
          Is only there.   Seventeenth century

Now may every living thing, young or old, weak or
    strong, living near or far, known or unknown, living
or departed or yet unborn, may every living thing be full   Buddha
of bliss.   Sixth century BCE

L o, the pious are in Gardens and delight,
Enjoying what their Lord hath bestowed upon them,
and their Lord hath protected them from the
punishment of the Hot Place.

Qur'an   Eat and drink with relish, for what ye have been doing.

M AY God give you of the dew of heaven,
and of the fatness of the earth,

Genesis 27:28   and plenty of grain and wine.

H AVING finished the Blue-plate Special
And reached the coffee stage,
Stirring her cup she sat,
A somewhat shapeless figure
Of indeterminate age
In an undistinguished hat.

When she lifted her eyes it was plain
That our globular furore,
Our international rout
Of sin and apparatus
And dying men galore,
Was not being bothered about.

Which of the seven heavens
Was responsible her smile
Wouldn't be sure but attested
That, whoever it was, a god
W. H. Auden   Worth kneeling-to for a while
Twentieth century   Had tabernacled and rested.

ALEX:

A h, in that case I know what I'll do.
I'm going to give you a little surprise:
You know, I'm rather a famous cook.
I'm going straight to your kitchen now
And I shall prepare you a nice little dinner
Which you can have alone. And then we'll leave you.
Meanwhile, you and Peter can go on talking
And I shan't disturb you.

EDWARD:

My dear Alex,
There'll be nothing in the larder worth your cooking.
I couldn't think of it.

ALEX:

Ah, but that's my special gift—
Concocting a toothsome meal out of nothing.
Any scraps you have will do. I learned that in the East.
With a handful of rice and a little dried fish
I can make half a dozen dishes. Don't say a word.
I shall begin at once.

T. S. Eliot
Twentieth century

F OR our sakes Christ became bread and wine, food and
drink. We make bold to eat him and to drink him. This
bread gives us solid and substantial strength. This wine
bestows courage, joy out of all earthly measure, sweetness,
beauty, limitless enlargement and perception. It brings life in
intoxicating excess, both to possess and to impart.

Romano Guardini
Twentieth century

Edward Foley
Kathleen Hughes
Gilbert Ostdiek
Twentieth century

TABLE-SHARING is only a moment in, and not the end of, the cycle of gift-exchange. The Eucharist of the future may need to give a much clearer witness that the life bestowed by the earth and human work and nurtured in the meal must be given for others and become productive in turn.

2 Kings 4:42–44

A man came from Baal-shalishah, bringing food from the first fruits to the man of God: twenty loaves of barley and fresh ears of grain in his sack. Elisha said, "Give it to the people and let them eat." But his servant said, "How can I set this before a hundred people?" So he repeated, "Give it to the people and let them eat, for thus says the LORD, 'They shall eat and have some left.'" He set it before them, they ate, and had some left, according to the word of the LORD.

Annie Dillard
Twentieth century

THIS is a spendthrift economy; though nothing is lost, all is spent.

Edith Sitwell
Twentieth century

PROCLAIM our Christ, and roar, "Let there be harvest! Let there be no more Poor—
For the Son of God is sowed in every furrow!"

THEY will question you concerning what they should expend. Say: "The abundance."

Qur'an

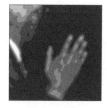

RABBI Hayyim had singled out certain poor people in his town, and gave them money every month. Not merely alms; he gave each what he required to support himself and his family.

On a certain market day a poultry dealer brought an unusually fine turkey to Zans. He took it straight to the rabbi's house and tried to sell it to his wife for the sabbath. But she thought it too dear, and so the man went off with his high-priced bird. A little later the woman found out that one of the men who received his sustenance from her husband had bought the turkey. "Now look at your poor!" she complained to the rabbi. "I wasn't able to buy the bird because the price was too high, but that man went and bought it!" "That shows," said the zaddik, "that he wants a good turkey as well for the sabbath. I didn't know that, but now that I do know it, I must raise the amount I give him every month."

Tales of the Hasidim
Eighteenth century

GOD answers our miserliness with abundance.

Jeffrey VanderWilt
Twentieth century

WHAT love is this of thine, that cannot be
     In thine infinity, O Lord, confined,
Unless it in thy very person see
     Infinity, and finity, conjoined?
     What! Hath thy Godhead, as not satisfied,
     Married our manhood, making it its bride?

Oh, matchless love! Filling Heaven to the brim!
     O'er-running it; all running o'er beside
This world! Nay, overflowing hell, wherein
     For thine elect there rose a mighty tide,
     That there our veins might through thy person bleed
     To quench those flames that else would on us feed!

Oh, that thy love might overflow my heart,
     To fire the same with love! For love I would.
But oh, my straitened breast! My lifeless spark!
     My fireless flame! What, chilly, love, and cold?
     In measure small? In manner chilly? See!
     Lord, blow the coal. Thy love inflame in me.

Edward Taylor
Seventeenth century

AND indeed," said Colonel Galliffet, "this woman is now turning a dinner at the Café Anglais into a kind of love affair—into a love affair of the noble and romantic category in which one no longer distinguishes between bodily and spiritual appetite or satiety!"

Isak Dinesen
Twentieth century

THE flesh feeds on the body and blood of Christ that the soul may be fattened on God.

Tertullian
Second century

WHEN the whole person is refreshed, this is abundant refreshment indeed.

Erasmus of Rotterdam
Sixteenth century

BARBECUING in my sackcloth.

The turkey is smoking well. The children have gone to bed, but they'll be up at dawn to open their presents.

The night is clear and cold. There is no moon. The light of the transmitter lies hard by Jupiter, ruby and diamond in the plush velvet sky. Ellen is busy in the kitchen fixing stuffing and sweet potatoes. Somewhere in the swamp a screech owl cries.

I'm dancing around to keep warm, hands in pockets. It is Christmas Day and the Lord is here, a holy night and surely that is all one needs.

Walker Percy
Twentieth century

I will make the whole earth my altar
and on it will offer you all the labors
   and sufferings of the world.

Teilhard de Chardin
Twentieth century

Nathan D. Mitchell
Twentieth century

EATING the eucharist is eating the world.

I s not this the fast that I choose:
        to loose the bonds of injustice,
    to undo the thongs of the yoke,
to let the oppressed go free,
    and to break every yoke?
Is it not to share your bread with the hungry,
    and bring the homeless poor into your house;
when you see the naked, to cover them,

Isaiah 58:6–7   and not to hide yourself from your own kin?

D o this: Be compassionate and then we may take the bread of compassion at eucharist with our whole soul and mind and heart. Being compassionate toward others, making neighbors of all people is the beginning of communion. We become the friends, the companions of God, those who break bread with God when we break open our lives

Megan McKenna   and care for the needs of our neighbors as our God has done
Twentieth century   with us.

S ome old men were entertaining themselves at Scetis by having a meal together; amongst them was Abba John. A venerable priest got up to offer drink, but nobody accepted any from him, except John the Dwarf. They were surprised and said to him, "How is it that you, the youngest, dared to let yourself be served by the priest?" Then he said to them, "When I get up to offer drink, I am glad when everyone accepts it, since I am receiving my reward; that is the reason, then, that I accepted it, so that he also might gain his reward and not be grieved by seeing that no-one would accept any-

Sayings of the   thing from him." When they heard this, they were all filled
Desert Fathers   with wonder and edification at his discretion.

L ORD Christ, we ask you to spread our table with your mercy. And may you bless with your gentle hands the good things you have given us. We know that whatever we have comes from your lavish heart, for all that is good comes from you. Thus whatever we eat, we should give thanks to you. And having received from your hands, let us give with equally generous hands to those who are poor, breaking bread and sharing our bread with them. For you have told us that whatever we give to the poor we give to you.

Alcuin of York
Eighth century

A true eucharist is never a passive, comforting moment alone with God, something which allows us to escape the cares and concerns of our everyday life. Eucharist is where all these cares and concerns come to a focus, and where we are asked to measure them against the standard lived by Jesus when he proclaimed for all to hear that the bread that he would give would provide life for the entire world. But it will do so only if, finding ourselves with a basket of bread, we have peered deeply enough into the heart of Christ to know what to do with it.

Paul Bernier
Twentieth century

T HE Samaritan went to him and bandaged his wounds, having poured oil and wine on them. Then he put him on his own animal, brought him to an inn, and took care of him. The next day he took out two denarii, gave them to the innkeeper, and said, "Take care of him; and when I come back, I will repay you whatever more you spend."

Luke 10:34–35

Flannery O'Connor
Twentieth century

Y ou will have found Christ when you are concerned with other people's sufferings and not your own.

Friedrich Heer
Twentieth century

D uring the session of 6 June, a high prelate showed the illustrious gathering a piece of black bread in order to arouse the pity of the Third Estate for the poor. He was interrupted by an unknown — Robespierre — with the words, "If your colleagues are so impatient to help the poor, then object to luxury, horses, carriages . . . and sell perhaps a fourth of the clerical estates. . . ."

Dietrich Bonhoeffer
Twentieth century

T he table fellowship of Christians implies obligation. It is *our* daily bread that we eat, not my own. We share our bread. Thus we are firmly bound to one another not only in the Spirit but in our whole physical being. The *one* bread that is given to our fellowship links us together in a firm covenant. Now none dares go hungry as long as another has bread, and he who breaks this fellowship of the physical life also breaks the fellowship of the Spirit.

THE story is told how on the Feast of Easter one year,
Oswald sat down to dine with Bishop Aidan. A silver
dish of rich food was set before him, and they were on the
point of raising their hands to bless the food, when the servant who was appointed to relieve the needs of the poor
came in suddenly and informed the king that a great crowd
of needy folk were sitting in the road outside begging alms
of the king. Oswald at once ordered his own food to be
taken out to the poor, and the silver dish to be broken up
and distributed among them.

Bede
Eighth century

THUS says God:
I will be heard!
Make flesh
of my every word:
give peace, justice, liberty
visible reality;
feed the hungry,
don't just meet
and plan
what they will one day eat.
Shelter the homeless,
help the poor,
the destitute,
the insecure.
Preach with your hands,
wear out your shoes:
words alone are not Good News.

Miriam Therese Winter
Twentieth century

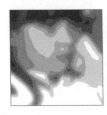

Eᴠᴇʀʏ day Euphemia took cooked food and bread and wine wherever anyone was confined or in prison or somewhere else. Indeed she went round all the squares of the city; and wherever she found someone ill or crippled or blind, or an old person unable to walk, she would sit down beside each in turn, asking, "What would you like today, dear? Would you just like me to buy you ordinary bread and some green vegetables? Or perhaps you would like something else; would you like me to go and buy you some fine white bread?" But whatever the reply and whoever it was who gave it, she would not leave him until she had satisfied him (when she went out, she always had her head covered). If she had no small change available, she would hurry home, take one of their utensils, and go out and pawn it, and so bring relief to that needy person.

Lives of the Eastern Saints
Sixth century

Oɴᴄᴇ on the Great Sabbath the rabbi of Roptchitz came home from the House of Prayer with weary steps. "What made you so tired?" asked his wife. "It was the sermon," he replied. "I had to speak of the poor and their many needs for the coming Passover, for unleavened bread and wine and everything else is terribly high this year."

"And what did you accomplish with your sermon?" his wife went on to ask.

"Half of what is necessary," he answered. "You see, the poor are now ready to take. As for the other half, whether the rich are ready to give—I don't know about that yet."

Tales of the Hasidim
Eighteenth century

THOSE who are generous are blessed,
for they share their bread with the poor.

Proverbs 22:9

THE eucharist and the poor are but one love for me.

Teresa of Calcutta
Twentieth century

FOR not only bread
but all things necessary
for sustenance in this life
are given on loan to us
   with others
   and because of others
   and for others
   to others through us.

Meister Eckhart
Thirteenth century

FOR though ye be true of your tongue and honestly earn,
And as chaste as a child that weepeth in church,
Unless ye love loyally and give to the poor,
Such goods as God sends you to them gladly giving,
Ye have no more merit in Mass or in hours
Than Malkin of her maidenhood that no man desireth.

William Langland
Fourteenth century

Anthony the Great
Fourth century

Our life and our death is with our neighbour.

Proverbs 25:21

If your enemies are hungry, give them bread to eat; and if they are thirsty, give them water to drink.

Matthew 10:42

Whoever gives even a cup of cold water to one of these little ones in the name of a disciple—truly I tell you, none of these will lose their reward.

Augustine of Hippo
Fourth century

If you wish to live in that good place where no one is hungry, now in this evil place break your bread with the hungry.

HE HAD BEEN MADE KNOWN TO THEM IN THE BREAKING OF
THE BREAD. Luke 24:35

~

W HEN he looked up and saw a large crowd coming towar him, Jesus said to Philip, "Where are we to buy bread for these people to eat?" He said this to test him, for he himself knew what he was going to do. Philip answered him, "Six months' wages would not buy enough bread for each of them to get a little." One of his disciples, Andrew, Simon Peter's brother, said to him, "There is a boy here who has five barley loaves and two fish. But what are they among so many people?" Jesus said, "Make the people sit down." Now there was a great deal of grass in the place; so they sat down, about five thousand in all. Then Jesus took the loaves, and when he had given thanks, he distributed them to those who were seated; so also the fish, as much as they wanted. When they were satisfied, he told the disciples, "Gather up the fragments left over, so that nothing may be lost." John 6:5 – 12

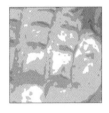

I am the bread of life. Your ancestors ate the manna in the wilderness, and they died. This is the bread that comes down from heaven, so that one may eat of it and not die. I am the living bread that came down from heaven. Whoever eats of this bread will live forever; and the bread that I will give for the life of the world is my flesh.

John 6:48 – 51

FOR as often as you eat this bread and drink the cup, you proclaim the Lord's death until he comes.

1 Corinthians 11:26

TANTUM ergo sacramentum
  Veneremur Cernui:
Et antiquum documentum
  Novo cedat ritui;
Praestet fides supplementum
  Sensuum defectui.

Thomas Aquinas
Thirteenth century

Notes

Scripture texts, except the psalms, are taken from *The New Revised Standard Version Bible*, 8 1989, Division of Christian Education of the National Council of the Churches of Christ in the United States of America. All rights reserved.

Excerpts from Psalms 23, 34, 42, 78 and 116 are from the English translation of the *Liturgical Psalter* © 1994, International Committee on English in the Liturgy, Inc. (ICEL). All rights reserved.

Hungering

Please, sir: from Charles Dickens, *Oliver Twist* (Penguin Books, 1975), p.56.

God of our: from the Baralong tribe, South Africa, in *Prayers of African Religion*. Used by permission of The Society for Promoting Christian Knowledge.

Ah, sir: from "The Second Shepherds' Pageant," in *Everyman and Medieval Miracle Plays* (New York: E. P. Dutton, 1959), p.86.

Our bodily: from Doris Janzen Longacre, *More-with-Less Cookbook* (Scottsdale, Penn.: Herald Press), p. 20.

During a period: from Martin Buber, *Tales of the Hasidim: The Later Masters* (New York: Schocken Books), p.128.

We cannot: from Elizabeth Dodson Gray, "New Earth Demands New Bread" in *Sacred Dimensions of Women's Experience* (Wellesley, Mass.: Round-table Press), p.170.

I have eaten: from Michael Quoist, *Prayers.* © Michael Quoist, 1963. Used by permission of Sheed & Ward.

The hungry: from John Milton, "Lycidas," in *The Norton Anthology of English Literature, Revised* (New York: W. W. Norton & Company, Inc., 1968), p. 1009.

The rat deserts: from Edith Sitwell, *The Canticle of the Rose* (New York: Vanguard Press, 1949), p. 143.

Let us sit: from Pablo Neruda, "The great table-cloth," as quoted in *The New Yorker,* June 24 & July 1, 1996, p. 68.

What lies: from Nathan D. Mitchell, *Eucharist as Sacrament of Initiation* (Chicago: Liturgy Training Publications, 1994) P. 50.

Here, then: from Saint Augustine, "Sermon 236" in *The Fathers of the Church* (New York: Fathers of the Church, Inc., 1959), p.234.

We may not: from *My Life for the Poor: Mother Teresa's Life and Work in Her Own Words* by Jose Luis Gonzalez-Balado and Janet N. Playfoot. Copyright © 1985 by Jose Luis Balado and Janet N. Playfoot. Reprinted by permission of HarperCollins Publishers, Inc.

I don't: from Nancy Mairs, *Ordinary Time* (Boston: Beacon Press, 1993), p. 89.

It seems to: from M. F. K. Fisher, *The Art of Eating.* © 1954 by M. F. K. Fisher. Used by permission of Macmillan Company.

Where is: from Charles Wesley, "Praying for Light and Assurance," in *John and Charles Wesley: Selected Prayers, Hymns, Journal Notes, Sermons, Letters and Treatises* (New York: Paulist Press, 1981), p.191.

I hunger: from song text by John S. B. Monsell, to "Hymn #413" in *Hymns Ancient & Modern, Revised* (Norwich, Norfolk: Hymns Ancient & Modern, Ltd., 1981), p. 562.

For truly: from Abba Poemen, in *The Sayings of the Desert Fathers* (Kalamazoo, Mich.: Cistercian Publications, 1975), p. 144.

When Helena: from Jerome, in *The Church fathers on the Bible,* Frank Sadowski, ed. (New York: Alba House, 1987), p. 191.

We hunger: from Romano Guardini, *Sacred Signs* (St. Louis: Pio Decimo Press, 1956), p. 66. Used by permission of Michael Glazier.

I yearn: from Dadu, in *The Oxford Book of Prayer,* George Appleton, ed. (England: Oxford University Press, 1985), p. 286.

My heart yearns: from a Zoroastrian prayer, quoted in *The Oxford Book of Prayer,* George Appleton, ed. (England: Oxford University Press, 1985), #32.

Hark Ho!: from *A Collection of Millennial Hymns Adapted to the Present Order of the Church* (New York: AMS Press, 1975), p. 19.

The ark of: Robert Farrar Capon, *Hunting the Divine Fox* (New York: Seabury Press, 1977), pp.164–165.

His strength: from Mary Herbert, "Psalm 147, 'Praise ye the Lord,'" in *The New Oxford Book of Christian Verse,* Donald Davie, ed. (England: Oxford University Press, 1981), p. 63.

Let the infinite: from Karl Rahner, *Meditations on the Sacraments* (New York: The Seabury Press, 1977), p. 40.

O Creator mine: from "O Creator mine! Thou hast created my heart for thyself alone, . . ." Sadhu Sundar Singh, p. 22 from *Morning Noon and Night,* edited by J Carden.

One day—it was: from *The Way of a Pilgrim,* translated from the Russian by R. M. French (New York: Seabury Press, 1965), p. 56.

They are at: from "A Baroque Wall Fountain in the Villa Sciarra" in *Things of This World,* copyright © 1955 and renewed 1983 by Richard Wilbur, reprinted by permission of Harcourt Brace & Company (and Faber and Faber Ltd. in the British Commonwealth, excluding Canada)

Gathering

Happens like this: from *Keeper'N Me* by Richard Wagamese © 1994. Reprinted with the permission of Doubleday Canada Limited.

What is this: from "WHAT IS THIS PLACE" Text and arrangement © 1967, Gooi en Stitch, bv., Baarn, The Netherlands. All rights reserved. Exclusive agent for English-language countries: OCP Publications, 5536 NE Hassalo, Portland OR 97213. All rights reserved. Used with permission.

In the windows: from Francis J. O'Malley, "The King of Heaven" in *O'Malley of Notre Dame* by John W. Meaney. © 1991 by University of Notre Dame Press. Used by permission of the publisher.

I had been: from Emily Dickinson, in *Final Harvest: Emily Dickinson's Poems,* Thomas H. Johnson, ed. (Boston: Little, Brown and Company, 1961), p. 147.

The bread is: from Robert Hovda, *It Is Your Own Mystery.* Copyright © 1977, The Liturgical Conference, 8750 Georgia Ave. Suite 123, Silver Spring MD 20910. All rights reserved. Used with permission.

There's no room: from Peggy Rosenthal, *Words and Values* (New York: Oxford University Press, 1984), p. 256.

The banquet: from Samuel Hooser, "Heavenly Feast," in *The Shaker Spiritual* by Daniel W. Patterson (Princeton N.J.: Princeton University Press, 1979), p. 178.

It cannot: from Balthasar Fischer, *Signs, Words & Gestures,* Matthew J. O'Connell, trans. (New York: Pueblo, 1981) p.72.

As baptised: from Mary Fabyan Windeatt, "Whom Shall We Love," in *Orate Fratres* 16 (1942). Used by permission of The Liturgical Press.

There is not: from Thomas Merton, *The Courage for Truth: The Letters of Thomas Merton to Writers,* Christine M. Bochen, ed. (San Diego: Harcourt Brace, 1994), p. 245.

Unequal in degree: from "Eight Riddles from Symphosius" in *Advice to a Prophet and Other Poems,* copyright © 1961 and renewed 1989 by Richard Wilbur, reprinted by permission of Harcourt Brace & Company (and Faber and Faber Ltd. in the British Commonwealth, excluding Canada).

She saw: from: "Revelation" from *Everything That Rises Must Converge* by Flannery O'Connor. Copyright ©1962, 1965 by the Estate of Mary Flannery O'Connor and copyright renewed © 1993 by Regina O'Connor. Reprinted by permission of Farrar, Straus & Giroux, Inc.

The eucharistic: from Robert Hovda, *It Is Your Own Mystery.* Copyright © 1977, The Liturgical Conference, 8750 Georgia Ave. Suite 123, Silver Spring MD 20910. All rights reserved. Used with permission.

Through this: from Karl Rahner, *Biblical Homilies* (New York: Herder and Herder, 1966), p. 34.

Let Mother Ecclesia: from Hildegard of Bingen, "Antiphon for Dedication of a Church," in *Symphonia,* trans. by Newman. Copyright 1988 by Cornell University Press. Used by permission.

I saw the throng: from Alice Meynell, "A General Communion," in *The New Oxford Book of Christian Verse,* Donald Davie, ed. (England: Oxford University Press, 1981), p. 251.

In one fresco: from Louis Zukofsky, *Complete Short Poetry.* © 1991 Paul Zukofsky. Used by permission of the Johns Hopkins university Press.

Food, like sex: Reprinted from *Models of God* by Sallie McFague, copyright © 1987 Fortress Press. Used by permission of Augsburg Fortress.

The Romans: from *Plutarch's Morality in Sixteen Volumes, IX,* Edwin L. Minar, Jr., F.H. Sandbach and W. C. Helmbold, trans. (Cambridge, Mass.: Harvard University Press, 1969), p. 5

When the sun: from Paphnutius, *Histories of the Monks of Upper Egypt and the Life of Onnophrius,* Tim Vivian, trans. (Kalamazoo, Mich.: Cistercian Publications, 1993), p.157.

If in other: from Plutarch, *Plutarch's Moralia, v. VII,* Paul A. Clement and Herbert B. Hoffleit, trans. (Cambridge, Mass.: Harvard University Press, 1969), pp. 31–32.

He, upon whom: from Pelagia, in *Holy Women of the Syrian Orient,* Sebastian P. Brock and Susan Ashbrook Harvey, trans. (Berkeley: University of California Press, 1987), pp. 48–49.

For God would: from John of the Cross, in *The Collected Works of St. John of the Cross,* Kieran Kavanaugh, OCD, and Otilio Rodriguez, OCD, trans. (Washington D.C.: ICS Publications, 1979), p. 728.

As Babbette's: from Isak Dinesen, "Babbette's Feast" in *Anecdotes of Destiny* © 1958 by Isak Dinesen. Used by permission of Vintage Books.

Wherein lies: from John Keats, "Endymion: A Poetic Romance," in *The Poems of John Keats,* Jack Stillinger, ed. (Cambridge Mass.: Belknap Press, 1978), ll. 77–81.

Next to her: from Nadine Gordimer, *Why Haven't You Written?* (England: Penguin Books, 1992), p. 199.

Come together: from *The Didache,* in Lucien Deiss, CSSp, *Springtime of the Liturgy,* Matthew J. O'Connell, trans. (Collegeville, Minn.: The Liturgical Press, 1979), p.77.

O lead: from William Ewart Gladstone, hymn text in *The English Hymnal with Tunes* (London: Oxford University Press, 1933), p. 454.

Do you know: from Levi Yitzhak, "Abraham and Lot," in *Tales of the Hasidim: The Early Masters* by Martin Buber (New York: Schocken Books, 1947), p.225.

Abba Pseleusius: from Paphnutius, *Histories of the Monks of Upper Egypt and The life of Onnophrius,* Tim Vivian, trans. (Kalamazoo, Mich.: Cistercian Publications, 1993), p. 76.

Alkínoös: from Homer, *The Odyssy,* Robert Fitzgerald, trans. (New York: Vintage Books, 1989), Book VII, ll. 171–176.

Love bade we: from George Herbert, "Love," in *The Works of George Herbert* (London: Oxford University Press, 1967), pp. 188–89.

Washed into: from "The Guest" from *Collected Poems: 1957–1982* by Wendell Berry. Copyright © 1985 by Wendell Berry. Reprinted by permission of North Point Press, a division of Farrar, Straus & Giroux, Inc.

We, this: fron Gail Ramshaw, *Words Around the Table* (Chicago: Liturgy Training Publications, 1991), p. 98.

The community: from Shawn Madigan, *Spirituality Rooted in Liturgy* (Washington, D. C.: The Pastoral Press, 1988), p. 111.

This was: Lyric excerpt of "A Real Nice Clambake" by Richard Rogers and Oscar Hammerstein II. Copyright © 1945 by Williamson Music, copyright renewed. International copyright secured. Reprinted by permission. All rights reserved.

Praying

Before the food: from *Keeper'N Me* by Richard Wagamese © 1994. Reprinted with the permission of Doubleday Canada Limited.

To God: from *Qur'an.*

Holy is God: from *Hermetic Corpus* in *Gnosticism: An Anthology,* R.N. Grant, Collins, eds. (London: Collins, 1961).

Great is: Zulu Nazarite Prayer, quoted in *The Oxford Book of Prayer* (Oxford: Oxford University Press, 1985), #159.

Small it is: by George Herbert, quoted in *The Oxford Book of Prayer* (Oxford: Oxford University Press, 1985), #10.

All you big: from "An African Canticle," pp. 47–48 from *Morning Noon and Night,* edited by J Carden. Used by permission of the Church Missionary Society.

The ancient: from William A. Anderson, *In His Light* (Dubuque, Iowa: Brown-Roa, 1996), p. 206.

At the last: from the English translation of the *Roman Missal* © 1973, International Committee on English in the Liturgy, Inc. (ICEL). All rights reserved.

We have: from John Chrysostom, *Sacraments and Worship* (Westminster, Maryland: Newman Press, 1955), p. 188.

The purpose: from Mark Searle, *Liturgy Made Simple,* © 1981. Used by permission of The Liturgical Press.

It is in public prayer: from Theodore W. Jennings Jr., "Prayer: The Call for God." Copyright 1981 Christian Century Foundation. Reprinted by permission from the April 15, 1981, issue of the *Christian Century.*

Since once: from Teilhard de Chardin, *La Messe Sur Le Monde,* quoted in *The Oxford Book of Prayer* (Oxford: Oxford University Press, 1985), p. 158–59.

Deck thyself: from Johann Franck, "Schmücke dich," in *Hymns Ancient and Modern, Revised* (Cambridge, England: Cambridge University Press, 1981), p. 531.

At the Lamb's: from R. Campbell, "Easter," in *Hymns Ancient & Modern,* Revised (England: Hymn Ancient & Modern, Ltd., 1981), p. 173.

The poor eat: from *Byzantine Daily Worship* (Allendale, New Jersey: Alleluia Press, 1969), p. 76.

We praise: from "We Praise You, God Almighty," quoted in *Springtime of the Liturgy,* by Lucien Deiss (Collegeville, Minnesota: Liturgical Press, 1979), p. 257.

Godhead here: from an anonymous thirteenth-century hymn, quoted in *The Oxford Book of Prayer* (Oxford: Oxford University Press, 1985), p. 157.

I have taken: From "Pryer After Eating" excerpted from *The Selected Poems of Wendell Berry,* Copyright © 1998 by Wendell Berry. Published by Counterpoint and reprinted by permission.

O Lord: from *The Prayer of the Faithful according to the Maronite Liturgical Year* (New York: Saint Maron Publications, 1984), p. 684. Used here with the permission of the copyright holder.

Yet the time: from Edith Sitwell, The Canticle of the Rose (New York: Vanguard Press, 1949), p. 149.

Draw nigh: from seventh-century Latin hymn "Sancti, venite, Christi Corpus sumite," *Hymns Ancient and Modern, Revised* (Cambridge, England: Cambridge University Press, 1981), p. 519

The one word: Reprinted with the permission of Scribner, a division of Simon & Schuster from *The Foreseeable Future* by Reynolds Price. Copyright © 1991 Reynolds Price.

There, there is: from "Charles Baudelaire: L'Invitation Au Voyage" in *Things of This World,* copyright 1956 and renewed 1984 by Richard Wilbur, reprinted by permission of Harcourt Brace & Company (and Faber and Faber Ltd. in the British Commonwealth, excluding Canada).

As he was dying: from *The Sayings of the Desert Fathers* (Kalamazoo, Michigan: Cistercian Publications, 1975), p. 37.

First, for the cup: from *Didache,* quoted in *Springtime of the Liturgy,* by Lucien Deiss (Collegeville, Minnesota: Liturgical Press, 1979), p. 74.

Then, after sharing: from Cyril of Jerusalem, quoted in *Springtime of the Liturgy,* by Lucien Deiss (Collegeville, Minnesota: Liturgical Press, 1979), p. 289.

Dear Miss Manners: from Judith Martin, *Miss Manners' Guide to Excruciatingly Correct Behavior* (New York: Warner Books, 1982) p. 128–129.

The table awaits: from Balthasar Fischer, *Signs, Words & Gestures* (New York: Pueblo, 1981), p. 31.

The meal: from Hippolytus of Rome, quoted in *The Macmillan Book of Earliest Christian Hymns* (New York: Macmillan Publishing Company, 1988), p. 68.

During the last: from Martin Buber, *Tales of the Hasidim* (New York: Schocken Books, 1947), pp. 261–62.

In the sacrament: from John F. Kavanaugh, *Following Christ in a Consumer Society* (Maryknoll, NY: Orbis Books, 1991), p.145. Used by permission.

In the Mass: from *My Life for the Poor: Mother Teresa's Life and Work in Her Own Words* by Jose Luis Gonzalez-Balado and Janet N. Playfoot. Copyright © 1985 by Jose Luis Balado and Janet N. Playfoot. Reprinted by permission of HarperCollins Publishers, Inc.

For you must: from Fyodor Dostoyevsky, *The Brothers Karamozov* (Baltimore: Penguin Books, 1958), p. 190.

Rabbi Mendel's: from Martin Buber, *Tales of the Hasidim* (New York: Schocken Books, 1947), p. 124.

Who offers: from Adé Bethune, quoted in *How Firm a Foundation: Voices of the Early Liturgical Movement* (Chicago: Liturgy Training Publications, 1990), p. 35.

Abba Isaiah also: from *The Sayings of the Desert Fathers* (Kalamazoo, Michigan: Cistercian Publications, 1975), p. 59.

When it was: from *The Little Flowers of St. Francis* (Garden City, New York: Image Books, 1958), p. 73.

To know: from John Henry Newman, quoted in *The Letters and Diaries of John Henry Newman* (London: Thomas Nelson and Sons, 1962), p. 224.

Let us: from the American folk hymn, "Let Us Break Bread Together," *Worship III* (Chicago: GIA, 1986), #727.

Bread-breakers: from Nathan Mitchell, *Eucharist as Sacrament of Initiation* (Chicago: Liturgy Training Publications, 1994), p. 143.

O salutaris: from Thomas Aquinas, *Worship III* (Chicago: GIA, 1986), #757.

Remembering

O Wealth: from Teresa of Avila, *Selected Writings of St. Teresa of Avila* (Milwaukee: Bruce Publishing Company, 1950), p. 57.

Father, we now: from the English translation of *The Roman Missal* © 1973, International Committee on English in the Liturgy, Inc. (ICEL). All rights reserved.

What he did: from the Corpus Christi Sequence taken from the *Roman Missal* approved by the National Conference for Catholic Bishops of the United States © 1964 by the National Catholic Welfare Conference, Inc. All rights reserved.

The eucharistic: from Mark Searle, *Liturgy Made Simple,* © 1981. Used by permission of The Liturgical Press.

Do you remember: from "THOSE CANAAN DAYS" from "Joseph and the Amazing Technicolor® Dreamcoat. Lyrics by Tim Rice, music by Andrew Lloyd Webber. © 1974 The Really Useful Group Ltd., London. All rights reserved. International copyright secured.

But what I: from Wendell Berry, *A World Lost* (Washington, DC: Counterpoint, 1996), p. 134. Used by permission.

As human beings: from William A. Anderson, *In His Light* (Dubuque, Iowa: Brown-Roa, 1996), p. 199.

According to thy: from James Montgomery, "According to Thy Gracious Word," *The Mennonite*

Hymnal (Scottsdale, Pennsylvania: Herald Press, 1969), #400.

The communities: from Robert N. Bellah, et al, *Habits of the Heart: Individualism and Commitment in American Life*. Copyright © 1985, 1996 Regents of the University of California.

We have lost: from Marge Piercy "The Common Living Dirt," from *Stone, Paper, Knife.* © 1983. Used by permission of Alfred A. Knopf.

The road was: from M. F. K. Fisher, *The Art of Eating.* © 1954 by M. F. K. Fisher. Used by permission of the Macmillan Company.

My aunt often: from Willa Cather, "My Mortal Enemy," in *Stories, Poems and Other Writings,* (New York: Viking Press, 1992).

My heart: from "My Heart, Being Hungry" by Edna St. Vincent Millay. From *Collected Poems,* HarperCollins. Copyright © 1923, 1951 by Edna St. Vincent Millay and Norma Millay Ellis. All rights reserved. Reprinted by permission of Elizabeth Barnett, literary executer.

The bread: Anonymous, quoted in *Early Christian Prayers* (Chicago: Henry Regnery, 1961), p. 137.

I know exactly: from Barbara Williamson, "Lamb of God," in *The Anglican Digest.*

Dying you: from the English translation of *The Roman Missal* © 1973, International Committee on English in the Liturgy, Inc. (ICEL). All rights reserved.

As often as: from the English translation of *The Roman Missal* © 1973, International Committee on English in the Liturgy, Inc. (ICEL). All rights reserved.

The real starting: from Evelyn Underhill, *Worship* (New York: Crossroad, 1984), p. 152.

This holy Mass: from Oscar Romero, in *A Martyr's Message of Hope: Six Homilies by Archbishop Oscar Romero* (Kansas City: Celebration Books, 1981), p. 166. Used by permission.

If it were: from Flannery O'Connor, *Everything That Rises Must Converge* (New York: Farrar, Straus and Giroux, 1975), p. xiii.

For this bread: from the Liturgy of Basil the Great, quoted in *The Oxford Book of Prayer* (Oxford: Oxford University Press, 1985), p. 230.

Come, O faithful ones: from the Orthodox liturgy in *Byzantine Daily Worship*. Used by permission of Alleluia Press, Allendale, NJ 07401.

This is the hour: from Horatius Bonar, "Here, O My Lord, I See Thee," *Lutheran Book of Worship* (Minneapolis: Augsburg, 1978), #211.

A second: from Nathan Mitchell, *Eucharist as Sacrament of Initiation* (Chicago: Liturgy Training Publications, 1994), p. 98.

We ate with: from "The Terrace" in *Ceremony and Other Poems,* copyright 1950 and renewed 1978 by Richard Wilbur, reprinted by permission of Harcourt Brace & Company (and Faber and Faber Ltd. in the British Commonwealth, excluding Canada).

From blossoms: from Pablo Neruda "Ode to the Lemon," in *Selected Odes of Pablo Neruda*. Edited/translated by Margaret Sayers Peden. Copyright © 1990 Regents of the University of California, © Fundacion Pablo Neruda.

Your noble: from Mechthild of Magdeburg, quoted in *Women Mystics in Medieval Europe* (New York: Paragon House, 1988), p. 60.

For sometimes: from the *Catechism of the Council of Trent for Parish Priests* (New York: Joseph Wagner, 1934), p. 214.

I've just: from the African-American spiritual "I've Just Come from the Fountain," *Lead Me, Guide Me* (Chicago: GIA, 1987), #110.

Only water: from Louis Zukofsky, *Complete Short Poetry.* © 1991 Paul Zukofsky. Used by permission of the Johns Hopkins University Press.

This feast: from Hippolytus of Rome, quoted in *The Macmillan Book of Earliest Christian Hymns* (New York: Macmillan Publishing Company, 1988), p. 66.

Let us praise: from W. H. Auden, "Anthem," in *W. H. Auden: Collected Poems.* © 1972 by W. H. Auden. Reprinted by permission of Random House, Inc.

The women kneeled: from Frank Waters, *The Man Who Killed the Deer* (New York: Washington Square Press, 1971), p. 33. Reprinted with the permission of Ohio University Press/Swallow Press, Athens, Ohio.

By eating: from Karl Rahner, *Meditations on the Sacraments*. Copyright © 1977 by the Seabury Press. Used by permission of the Crossroad Publishing Company.

And then: from Robert Browning, *Robert Browning: The Poems,* Volume 1 (New Haven, Connecticut: Yale University Press, 1981), p. 415.

Anima Christi: from an anonymous fourteenth-century hymn, in *The Hymns of the Breviary and Missal.* (New York: Benzinger Brothers, 1922), p. 193.

Lord Jesus: from the English translation of *The Roman Missal* © 1973, International Committee on English in the Liturgy, Inc. (ICEL). All rights reserved.

On the day: from Martin Buber, *Tales of the Hasidim* (New York: Schocken Books, 1947), p. 120.

Now the green: "Now the green blade rises" (verse 1), words by JMC Crum, in *The Oxford Book of Carols*. Used by permission of Oxford University Press.

Offering

Now Christ: from a Latin hymn in *The English Hymnal* (London: Oxford University Press, 1933), p. 179.

Little Lamb: from William Blake, quoted in The *Norton Anthology of English Literature,* fourth edition, volume 1 (New York: W.W. Norton & Company, 1979), p. 32.

Did he: from William Blake, quoted in *The Norton Anthology of English Literature,* fourth edition, volume 1 (New York: W.W. Norton & Company, 1979), p. 40.

Sacrificing an animal: from Margaret Visser, *The Rituals of Dinner,* 1991 by Margaret Visser. Used by permission of Grove/Atlantic, Inc.

Sing, my tongue: from Thomas Aquinas, "Sing, my tongue," in *The Catholic Hymnal and Service Book* (New York: Benzinger Editions, 1966), #241.

Very merrily: from Julian of Norwich, *Julian of Norwich: Showings* (New York: Paulist Press, 1978), p. 146.

The shepherd says: from John of the Cross, *The Collected Works of St. John of the Cross* (Washington, D.C.: ICS Publications, 1979), p. 722.

Look with favor: from the English translation of The Roman Missal © 1973, International Committee on English in the Liturgy, Inc. (ICEL). All rights reserved.

That the oblation: from Pius XII, quoted in *Sacraments and Worship* (Westminster, Maryland: Newman Press, 1955), p. 213.

And here: from the *First Prayer Book of Edward VI,* quoted in *Sacraments and Worship* (Westminster, Maryland: Newman Press, 1955), p. 204.

The oblation: from Evelyn Underhill, *Worship* (New York: Crossroad, 1984), p. 161.

Hail, altar: from Fortunatus, "Pange lingua," quoted in *The Macmillan Book of Earliest Christian Hymns* (New York: Macmillan Publishing Company, 1988), p. 220.

He is the true: from the English translation of *The Roman Missal* © 1973, International Committee on English in the Liturgy, Inc. (ICEL). All rights reserved.

You, O lord: from *Qurbono: The Book of Offering* (New York: Saint Maron Publications, 1994), p. 113. Used here with the permission of the copyright holder.

He is the tender: from Angela Carter. "The Erl-King" from *The Bloody Chamber and Other Adult Tales* (New York: HarperCollins, 1979).

The Word: from Thomas Aquinas, quoted in *The Liturgy of the Hours,* Volume III (New York: Catholic Book Publishing, 1975), p. 604.

The dripping: from "East Coker" in *Four Quartets,* copyright 1943 by T.S. Eliot and renewed 1971 by Esme Valerie Eliot, reprinted by permission of Harcourt Brace & Company (U.S.) and Faber and Faber Ltd. (outside U.S.).

Lord of the Powers: from Serapion of Thmuis, quoted in *Springtime of the Liturgy,* by Lucien Deiss (Collegeville, Minnesota: Liturgical Press, 1979), pp. 194–95.

In this sad: from Edward Taylor, "Meditation Eight, First Series," quoted in *The Literature of Early America* (Columbus, Ohio: Charles E. Merrill Books, 1967), p. 197.

Pentecost and fire: from Jeffrey VanderWilt, "The Holy Spirit of God."

Let me be fodder: from Ignatius of Antioch, quoted in *Early Christian Fathers* (New York: Macmillan, 1970), p. 104.

Our life: from Sister Jane Walker, OP, "Sketch of Our Congregation's Charism," © 1975, Eucharistic Missionaries of St. Dominic, New Orleans, LA.

Tears are dried: from Anita M. Constance, S.C., *A Time to Turn . . . The Paschal Experience.* Copyright © 1995 by Sisters of Charity. Used by Permission of Paulist Press.

Blessed are you: from the English translation of *The Roman Missal* © 1973, International Committee on English in the Liturgy, Inc. (ICEL). All rights reserved.

Consecrate this: from *Qurbono: The Book of Offering* (New York: Saint Maron Publications, 1994), p. 170. Used here with the permission of the copyright holder.

Fill high: from John Keble, "Fill High the Bowl," quoted in *The New Oxford Book of Christian Verse* (Oxford: Oxford University Press, 1981), p. 217.

An ancient: from Margaret Visser, *The Rituals of Dinner,* © 1991 by Margaret Visser. Used by permission of Grove/Atlantic, Inc.

In the dark: from James Baldwin, "Sonny's Blues," in *The Story and Its Writer: An Introduction to Short Fiction,* Ann Charters (Boston: Bedford Books, 1995).

Come slowly: from Emily Dickinson, "44," *Final Harvest* (Boston: Little, Brown & Company, 1890), p. 24.

To drink: from Clement of Alexandria, quoted in *The Early Christian Fathers* (Oxford: Oxford University Press, 1969), p. 181.

By this they: from Clement of Rome, quoted in *Early Christian Fathers* (New York: Macmillan, 1970), p. 49.

Would you: from Lewis Jones, "Would You Be Free," in *The Mennonite Hymnal* (Scottsdale, Pennsylvania: Herald Press, 1969), # 555.

Your blood: Hippolytus of Rome, quoted in *The Macmillan Book of Earliest Christian Hymns* (New York: Macmillan Publishing Company, 1988), p. 66.

Blood of Jesus: Anonymous, quoted in *Springtime of the Liturgy*, by Lucien Deiss (Collegeville, Minnesota: Liturgical Press, 1979), p. 259.

You are there: from Augustine of Hippo, *Commentary on the Lord's Sermon on the Mount* (New York: Fathers of the Church, 1951), pp. 322–23.

But this thing: from Louis Zukofsky, *Complete Short Poetry*. © 1991 Paul Zukofsky. Used by permission of the Johns Hopkins University Press.

When the roast: from Willa Cather, *A Lost Lady*. Copyright © 1923 by Willa Cather, renewed 1951 by the executors of the Estate of Willa Cather.

Then they restored: from Proba, quoted in *A Lost Tradition* (Lanham, Maryland: University Press of America, 1981), p. 65.

Ben knew: from *The Boy Who Could Sing Pictures* by Seymour Leichman. Copyright ©1968 by Seymour Leichman. Used by permission of Bantam Doubleday Dell Books for Young Readers.

God has: from Mechthild of Magdeburg, *Meditations with Mechthild of Magdeburg* (Santa Fe, New Mexico: Bear & Company, 1982), p. 56.

Eating and Drinking

On the night: from Thomas Aquinas, "Sing, my tongue," in *The Catholic Hymnal and Service Book* (New York: Benzinger Editions, 1966), #241.

We wouldn't: from Joseph Campbell, quoted on *Joseph Campbell and the Power of Myth with Bill Moyers*, "Program 5: Love and the Goddess."

Since Eve: from Lord Byron, *Don Juan*. Public Domain.

Then the big part: from *Keeper'N Me* by Richard Wagamese © 1994. Reprinted with the permission of Doubleday Canada Limited.

Gilgamesh, fill: from *The Epic of Gilgamesh*. Public Domain.

The Lord gave: from Karl Rahner, *Meditations on the Sacraments* New York: Seabury Press, 1977), p. 35.

Art is a matter: from *Willa Cather in Person: Interviews, Speeches, and Letters*, edited by L. Brent Bohlke. University of Nebraska Press, 1986.

And Eve, within: from John Milton, *Paradise Lost*. Public Domain.

The work done: from Homer, *The Iliad, Book I*. Public Domain.

Rev. J. B. Schlund's: from the recipe book of David A. Woods.

Alleluia! Bread: from William C. Dix, "Alleluia! Sing to Jesus," in *Worship* (Chicago: GIA, 1986) #737.

You satisfy: from Omer Westendorf, "You Satisfy the Hungry Heart." Public Domain.

O God, you fed: from Ulrich Zwingli, in *Prayers of the Eucharist: Early and Reformed*, trans. and ed. by R.C.D. Jasper and G.J. Cuming (New York: Oxford University Press, 1980), p. 131.

We taste thee: attributed to Bernard of Clairvaux, "Jesu, dulcedo cordium," in *Hymns Ancient and Modern, Revised*, Full score edition (Great Britain: Hymns Ancient & Modern, Ltd., 1981) #387.

Eat this bread: from "Eat this bread," © 1984 by les presses de Taize (France). Used by permission of G.I.A. Publications, Inc., exclusive agent. All rights reserved.

Who would suppose: from Lord Byron, *Don Juan*, Canto XV. Public Domain.

You probably need: from CATHEDRAL by Raymond Carver. Copyright © 1981 by Raymond Carver. Reprinted by permission of Alfred A. Knopf Inc.

If we understand: from Paul Bernier, *Bread Broken and Shared* (Notre Dame: Ave Maria Press, 1981), p. 75. Used by permission of Paul Bernier.

He chooses to: from Robert Griffin, *I Never Said I Didn't Love You* (Laurel, Md.: Paulist Press, 1977), p. 81.

There feeding: from Augustine of Hippo, in *The Fathers of the Church* (New York: The Fathers of the Church, Inc., 1959), p. 27.

As honey: from "The Odes of Solomon" in *The Earliest Christian Hymns* (New York: Macmillan Publishing, 1988), p. 55.

This Earth is: from Edith Sitwell, *The Canticle of the Rose* (New York: Vanguard Press, 1949), p. 238.

The pedigree: from Emily Dickinson, "544" in *Final Harvest: Emily Dickinson's Poems* (Boston: Little, Brown and Company, 1961), p. 306.

Surrounded by clay: from Eduardo Galeano, *Memory of Fire, II Faces and Masks*, tr. Cedric Belfrage (New York: Pantheon Books, 1987).

Heaped up: from Charles Dickens, *A Christmas Carol* (New York: Airmont Publishing, 1963), p. 65.

Let my Beloved: from Isaac Watts, "The Church the Garden of Christ," in *The New Oxford Book of Christian Verse* (New York: Oxford University Press, 1981), p. 148.

He makes: from Andrew Marvell, "Bermudas," in *The New Oxford Book of Christian Verse* (New York: Oxford University Press, 1981), p. 111.

As the vintages: from Francis Thompson, "To a Poet Breaking Silence," in *The Works of Francis Thompson, Poems: Volume I* (New York: AMS Press, 1970), p. 81.

I taste: from Emily Dickinson, "46" in *Final Harvest: Emily Dickinson's Poems* (Boston: Little, Brown and Company, 1962), p. 25.

Wine possesses: from Romano Guardini, *Sacred Signs* (St. Louis: Pio Decimo Press, 1956), p. 66. Used by permission of Michael Glazier.

In the inner: from John of the Cross, in *The Collected Works of St. John of the Cross,* Kieran Kavanaugh, OCD, and Otilio Rodriguez, OCD, trans. (Washington D.C.: ICS Publications, 1979), p. 714.

All the same: from Isak Dinesen, "Babbette's Feast" in *Anecdotes of Destiny* © 1958 by Isak Dinesen. Used by permission of Vintage Books.

Come, O faithful: from the Orthodox liturgy in *Byzantine Daily Worship.* Used by permission of Alleluia Press, Allendale, NJ 07401.

Come, let us: from John Damascene, translated by J. M. Neale in *The English Hymnal with Tunes* (London: Oxford University Press, 1960) #138.

While yet: from Ephrem in *The Sayings of the Desert Fathers* (Kalamazoo, Mich.: Cistercian Publications, 1975), p. 50.

So the priest: from *The Little Flowers of St. Francis* (Garden City, New York: Image Books, 1958), p. 85.

Our life: from Sister Jane Walker, OP, "Sketch of Our Congregation's Charism," © 1975, Eucharistic Missionaries of St. Dominic, New Orleans, LA.

I would like: from a Celtic poem, "The Heavenly Banquet," in *Daily Readings from Prayers & Praises in the Celtic Tradition* (Springfield, Ill.: Templegate Publishers, 1986), p. 58.

Greet chiere: from Geoffrey Chaucer, *The Canterbury Tales,* in *The Riverside Chaucer* (Boston: Houghton Mifflin, 1987), p. 35.

While spoon-feeding: Excerpt from "Parkinson's Disease," from *Imperfect Thirst* by Galway Kinnell. Reprinted by permission of Houghton Mifflin Company. All rights reserved.

On the table: from Nathan D. Mitchell, *Eucharist as Sacrament of Initiation* (Chicago: Liturgy Training Publications, 1993), p. 56.

During the retreat: Excerpt from *Dakota.* Copyright © 1993 by Kathleen Norris. Reprinted by permission of Ticknor & Fields/Houghton Mifflin Co. All rights reserved.

Very bread: from the Corpus Christi Sequence taken from the *Roman Missal* approved by the National Conference for Catholic Bishops of the United States © 1964 by the National Catholic Welfare Conference, Inc. All rights reserved.

Healing

For, ere: from "Let us employ all notes of joy" by Adam Fox, © Hope Publishing Co., Carol Stream, IL 60188. All rights reserved. Used by permission.

Your death: from Karl Rahner, *Prayers for a Lifetime,* ed. Albert Raffelt. Copyright © 1987 by The Crossroad Publishing Company. Used by permission.

I am: from *Pilgrim at Tinker Creek* by Annie Dillard. Copyright © 1974 by Annie Dillard. Reprinted by permission of HarperCollins Publishers, Inc.

Hail, saving: from Ambrose of Milan, quoted in *Saint Joseph Daily Missal* (New York: Catholic Book Publishing Co., 1959).

God has created: from Julian of Norwich, in *Julian of Norwich: Showings* (New York: Paulist Press, 1978), p. 137.

For Jesus shed: from John Hart Stockton, "Come, Every Soul by Sin Oppressed," in *The Mennonite Hymnal* (Scottsdale, Penn.: Herald Press, 1969), #553.

The dying: from William Cowper, in *The English Hymnal with Tunes* (London: Oxford University Press, 1933), #332.

Oh, purer than: from Sedulius, "Credelis Herodes Deum," in *Earliest Christian Hymns* (New York: Macmillan Publishing Company, 1988), p. 212.

Cancel out: from Catherine of Siena, "Prayer 8," in *The Prayers of Catherine Siena* (New York: Paulist Press, 1983), p. 65.

He breaks: from Charles Wesley, in *John and Charles Wesley: Selected Prayers, Hymns, Journal Notes, Sermons, Letters and Treatises* (New York: Paulist Press, 1981), p. 178.

You bought us: from an anonymous prayer in *Early Christian Prayers* (Chicago: Henry Regnery Co., 1962), p. 67.

I'd prefer: from Trevor Joyce, *Stone Floods* (Dublin: New Writers' Press, 1995), p. 52. Used by permission.

Evil has power: from Tim Vivian, *Histories of the Monks of Upper Egypt* (Kalamazoo, Mich.: Cistercian Publications, 1993), p.29.

Anyone who enters: from Norman Pittenger, *Life as Eucharist* (Grand Rapids, Mich.: William B. Eerdmans, 1973), p. 62.

The two old women: from Isak Dinesen, "Babbette's Feast" in *Anecdotes of Destiny* © 1958 by Isak Dinesen. Used by permission of Vintage Books.

Two youths who: from Martin Buber, *Tales of the Hasidim* (New York: Schocken Books, 1948), pp. 194–95.

The rood of: from Nathan D. Mitchell, *Eucharist as Sacrament of Initiation* (Chicago: Liturgy Training Publications, 1993), pp. 41–42.

So you plan: from Walker Percy, *Lancelot* (New York: Farrar, Straus and Giroux, 1976), p. 256.

I am not: from John Chrysostom, quoted in *The Oxford Book of Prayer*, George Appleton, ed. (England: Oxford University Press, 1985), #524.

Break one loaf: from Ignatius of Antioch, in *Early Christian Fathers* (New york: The Macmillan Company, 1972), p.93.

Let us therefore: from John Calvin, in *Prayers of the Eucharist: Early and Reformed* (New York: Oxford University Press, 1980), p. 155.

Here let each: from John Huss, *"Jesus Christus, nostra salus,"* in *The Catholic Hymnal and Service Book* (new York: Benziger Editions, 1966), #177.

That daily bread: from Ambrose of Milan, quoted in *Catechism of the Council of Trent for Parish Priests* (New York: Joseph F. Wagner, Inc., 1934), p. 244.

Blood that bled: from Hildegard of Bingen, *Saint Hildegard of Bingen: Symphonia* (Ithaca: Cornell University Press, 1988), p. 103.

He drank some: from Iris Murdoch, A Fairly Honorable Defeat (England: Penguin Books, 1970), p. 437.

Lucy Texada Roberts': from Anne B. Parks.

O God of Truth: from Serapion of Thmuis, in *Sacraments and Worship: Liturgy and Doctrinal Development of Baptism, Confirmation, and the Eucharist* (Westminster, Md.: The Newman Press, 1955), p. 44.

To heal the: from "A Baghdad Cookery Book," quoted in *Acquired Taste: The French Origins of Modern Cooking* (Ithaca: Cornell University Press, 1994), p. 17.

From at least: from T. Sarah Peterson, *Acquired Taste: The French Origins of Modern Cooking* (Ithaca: Cornell University Press, 1994), p. xiv.

Then St. francis: from *The Little Flowers of St. Francis* (New York: Image Books, 1958), p. 98.

It was said: from *The Sayings of the Desert Fathers* (Kalamazoo, Mich.: Cistercian Publications, 1975), p. 92.

May I become: from Santideva, *The Path of Light.*

In these acts: from Leo the Great.

No picnic party: from *My Son's Story* by Nadine Gordimer. Copyright © 1990 by Felix Licensing B.V.

Reprinted by permission of Farrar, Straus & Giroux, Inc.

One of the crowd: from Alice Meynell, "The Unknown God," *Alice Meynell: Prose and Poetry* (Freeport, N.Y.: Books for Libraries Press, 1970), p. 372.

The abundance: from "Work Song" Excerpted from *Clearing,* copyright © 1977 by Wendell Berry. Published by Harcourt Brace and reprinted by permission of the author.

Come, my Light: from Dimitrii of Rostov, in *The Orthodox Way* by Kalistos Ware, (NY: St. Vladimir's Seminary Press, 1995).

Almighty, everlasting: from Thomas Aquinas, quoted in *The Oxford Book of Prayer*, George Appleton, ed. (England: Oxford University Press, 1985), #519.

Strengthen, O Lord: from the Liturgy of Malabar, quoted in *The Oxford Book of Prayer*, George Appleton, ed. (England: Oxford University Press, 1985), #527.

Feeding the World

It prospered: from George Herbert, "Peace," in *The New Oxford Book of Christian Verse* (New York: Oxford University Press, 1981), p.85.

Now may every: from Buddha, quoted in *The Oxford Book of Prayer*, George Appleton, ed. (England: Oxford University Press, 1985), #1118.

Lo, the pious: from *The Qur'an.*

Having finished: From W. H. Auden, "In Schrafft's," in *W. H. Auden: Collected Poems* © 1949 by W. H. Auden. Used by permission of Random House, Inc.

Alex: from *The Cocktail Party,* copyright 1950 by T.S. Eliot and renewed 1978 by Esme Valerie Eliot, reprinted by permission of Harcourt Brace & Company.

For our sakes: from Romano Guardini, *Sacred Signs* (St. Louis: Pio Decimo Press, 1956), p. 66. Used by permission of Michael Glazier.

Table-sharing is: from Edward Foley, Kathleen Hughes, Gilbert Ostdiek, "The Preparatory Rites: A Case Study in Liturgical Ecology," *Worship,* v. 67 (January 1993), p. 36

This is a spendthrift: from Annie Dillard, *Pilgrim at Tinker Creek* (New York: HarperPerennial, 1974), p. 65.

Proclaim Christ: from Edith Sitwell, *The Canticle of the Rose* (New York: Vanguard Press, 1949), p. 274.

They will: from the *Qur'an.*

Rabbi Hayyim: from Martin Buber, *Tales of the Hasidim* (New York: Schocken Books, 1948), p. 211.

God answers: from Jeffrey VanderWilt, "Loaves and Fish, the Meals of Jesus."

What love is: from Edward Taylor, "Preparatory Meditations Before My Approach to the Lord's Supper," *The Poems of Edward Taylor* (New Haven: Yale University Press, 1963).

And indeed: from Isak Dinesen, "Babbette's Feast" in *Anecdotes of Destiny* © 1958 by Isak Dinesen. Used by permission of Vintage Books.

The flesh feeds: from Tertullian, "De Resurrectione Carnis, 8," quoted in *The Early Christian Fathers* (New York: Oxford University Press, 1969), p. 148.

When the whole: from Erasmus of Rotterdam, *Ten Colloquies* (New York: The Bobbs-Merrill Co., Inc., 1957), p. 150.

Barbecuing in my: from Walker Percy, *Love in the Ruins,* © 1971 by Walker Percy. Used by permission of Farrar, Straus & Giroux, Inc.

I will make: Reprinted with permission from *Meditations with Teilhard de Chardin,* by Blanche Gallagher, copyright 1988, Bear & Co., Santa Fe, NM.

Eating the eucharist: from Nathan D. Mitchell, *Eucharist as Sacrament of Initiation* (Chicago: Liturgy Training Publications, 1994), p. 112.

Do this: from Megan McKenna, *Parables: The Arrows of God* (Maryknoll, NY: Orbis Books, 1994), p. 151. Used by permission.

Some old men: from *Sayings of the Desert Fathers* (Kalamazoo, Mich.: Cistrcian Publications, 1975), p. 74.

Lord Christ, we: from Alcuin of York, quoted in *The HarperCollins Book of Prayers* (New York: Harper-Collins, 1993), p. 22.

A true Eucharist: from Paul Bernier, *Bread Broken and Shared* (Notre Dame: Ave Maria Press, 1981), pp.139–40. Used by permission of Paul Bernier.

You will have: from Flannery O'Connor, *The Habit of Being* (New York: Vintage Books, 1979), p. 453.

During the session: from Friedrich Heer, *The Intellectual History of Europe,* trans., Jonathan Steinberg (Cleveland: World Publishing Company, 1966), p.405.

The table: from *Life Together* by Dietrich Bonhoeffer. English translation copyright © 1954 by Harper & Brothers, Copyright renewed 1982 by Helen S. Doberstein. Reprinted by permission of Harper-Collins Publishers, Inc.

The story is told: from Bede, *A History of the English Church and People* (England: Penguin Books, 1974), p. 150.

Thus says God: from Miriam Therese Winter, *Woman Prayer, Woman Song.* © 1987 by The Medical Mission Sisters. Used by permission.

Every day: from Euphemia, in *Lives of the Eastern Saints,* quoted in *Holy Women of the Syrian Orient* (Berkeley: University of California Press, 1987), pp. 126–27.

Once on the: from Martin Buber, *Tales of the Hasidim* (New York: Schocken Books, 1948), p. 197.

The Eucharist: from *My Life for the Poor: Mother Teresa's Life and Work in Her Own Words* by Jose Luis Gonzalez-Balado and Janet N. Playfoot. Copyright © 1985 by Jose Luis Balado and Janet N. Playfoot. Reprinted by permission of HarperCollins Publishers, Inc.

For not only: from Meister Eckhart. Public Domain.

For though ye: from William Langland, "Good Works," quoted in *The New Oxford Book of Christian Verse* (New York: oxford University Press, 1981) p. 11.

Our life: from Anthony the Great, in *The Sayings of the Desert Fathers* (Kalamazoo, Mich.: Cistercian Publications, 1975), p. 2.

If you wish: from Augustine of Hippo, quoted in *The Fathers of the Church* (New York: the Fathers of the Church, Inc., 1958), p. 162.

Tantum ergo: from Thomas Aquinas, "Pange Lingua."

Author/Source Index